TWAYNE'S
RULERS AND STATESMEN OF THE WORLD SERIES

Hans L. Trefousse, Brooklyn College
General Editor

JOSEPH II

(TROW 5)

Joseph II

By PAUL P. BERNARD

Colorado College

Twayne Publishers, Inc. :: New York

To my parents

tennen show 8

SOS   38-30

wallet

Body lotion

tresor   La Cou

ear rings   Gold
nona

lamp nichm Brass

Preface

THIS BOOK DOES NOT PRETEND TO BE THE MAJOR BIOGRAPHY IN English which Emperor Joseph II so amply deserves. Such a biography would require three or four times the number of pages allotted to books in the present series. Aside from certain aspects of Joseph's foreign policy and the ideological roots of Josephinism, this book is not based on archival resources but rather on a, hopefully thorough, reading of the published literature. As a result, it is necessarily uneven. The last two decades have seen the publication of a flood of materials dealing with Joseph's religious policies, with Professor Maass' gigantic work occupying pride of place among these; good work has also been done on Austrian intellectual history of the period, but the economic history of Joseph's reign still rests on the assumptions which were fashionable at the beginning of the century, when Mitrofanov wrote. Only very lately has an occasional journal article demonstrated that in this area there are not only new interpretations but also new materials to be found. I have tried to make a coherent story out of these necessarily disparate materials. The notes should not be regarded as a full-fledged scholarly apparatus. Except in cases where they are meant to correct blatant errors of fact or interpretation in other studies, they serve merely to draw attention to more detailed treatments of certain subjects or to refer the reader to important passages in the correspondence of the *dramatis personae*.

I owe a debt of gratitude to my colleague Bentley Gilbert, who read several chapters in manuscript; to my colleague William Hochman, who encouraged me to undertake this work; to Professor Günther Hamann of the University of Vienna, who gave me the benefit of his discerning opinions of Joseph; to Professor Hermann Freudenberger of Tulane University, who gave me much sound advice in economic questions; to Professor S. Harrison Thomson, who first led me out into the treacherous field of Central European History and showed me the signposts. The responsibility for whatever errors this work may contain, is of course solely mine.

Contents

Chronology

1740 Succession of Maria Theresia and outbreak of First Silesian War.
1741 Birth of Joseph.
1748 Treaty of Aix-la-Chapelle. Silesia is lost.
1756–63 Seven Years' War
1760 Joseph marries Isabella of Parma.
1761 Joseph submits first memorandum on government to Maria Theresia.
1762 Birth of Joseph's daughter Maria Theresia.
1763 Death of Isabella.
1764 Joseph crowned King of the Romans.
1765 Joseph marries Josepha of Bavaria.
Death of Emperor Francis Stephen. Joseph appointed co-regent. Submission of second memorandum on government.
1766 First law regulating amount of *robot* due from peasants.
1767 Death of Josepha.
1768 Publication of *Nemesis Theresiana*.
1769 Joseph's visit to Rome. Meeting of Joseph and Frederick II of Prussia at Neustadt.
1770 Death of Joseph's daughter Maria Theresia. Meeting of Joseph and Frederick II at Neisse.
1771 Creation of first Urbarial Commission. Joseph's visit to Bohemia.
1772 First partition of Poland.
1773 Dissolution of the Society of Jesus.
1774 First Urbarial Patent. Joseph's first visit to France.
1775 Peasant rebellion in Bohemia.
1777 Joseph's declaration on religious toleration.
1778–79 War of the Bavarian Succession.
1780 Joseph's first visit to Russia. Austro-Russian Treaty. Death of Maria Theresia, Joseph becomes sole ruler.
1781 Joseph's second visit to France. First Josephinian law code promulgated. Creation of government censorship commission. Edict of Toleration. Abolition of formal serfdom.

1782   Creation of Commission to supervise spiritual affairs. Dissolution of the monasteries. Visit of Pope Pius VI to Vienna.

1783   Second visit of Joseph to Rome. Decree for commutation of *robot* into money payments.

1784   Joseph's Concordate with Rome. Quarrel with Holland over the closing of the Scheldt.

1784–85   Attempts to exchange the Austrian Netherlands for Bavaria.

1785   Creation of commission to survey and register all land.

1786   Abolition of craft guilds. Death of Frederick II.

1787   General reform of criminal law. Second visit of Joseph to Russia. Revolt in the Austrian Netherlands.

1787–89   Austro-Russian war against Turkey.

1789   Abolition of *robot* and introduction of general tax on land. Repeal of administrative reforms in Hungary. Renewed revolt in Austrian Netherlands.

1790   Death of Joseph.

CHAPTER I

The Advent of a Prince

DYNASTIES, WITH FEW EXCEPTIONS, HAVE BEEN SENSITIVE TO THE lack of a male heir. This is not to say that a woman, once enthroned, is unable to control and direct the elaborate machinery associated with an absolute monarchy. Examples to the contrary abound, but the prospect of a female ruler usually does not inspire confidence. Assorted pirates, pretenders, and parvenus have often been encouraged to embark on schemes which they hitherto had been constrained to keep locked up in their dissident breasts. Thus, the accession to the throne of Maria Theresia upon the death of the Emperor Charles VI in 1740 provoked not only an instantaneous Prussian descent upon the Austrian province of Silesia, but also alarming dissension in other parts of Austria. The Pragmatic Sanction, guaranteeing the indivisibility of the Austrian dominions, was now, it seemed, a dead letter, in spite of the fact that Charles had devoted so large a portion of his energies and so much of his money to secure its acceptance by the principal powers of Europe. No power came to the aid of Austria against Frederick II. The German Electors refused to cast their votes for Maria Theresia's husband, Francis Stephen, formerly Duke of Lorraine, who had recently been consoled for the loss of that rich and progressive land with the rather empty title of Grand Duke of Tuscany. Even in the hereditary domains of the House of Hapsburg, the Estates were holding back, not supporting the war effort, speculating whether they might not be handsomely rewarded by whoever should succeed in smashing Austria to pieces.[1] In Vienna circumspect members of the high nobility, the already formidable Prince Kaunitz for one, pleaded illness, *force majeure,* or whatever came to their minds in order to escape appointments which would identify them too closely with a tottering throne.

As if all this were not trouble enough, Maria Theresia had since her marriage given birth to three daughters. The seed of Hapsburg, so vigorous over the last five centuries, seemed at last to be weakening. In 1741 the Archduchess was pregnant again. It

[13]

was, to be sure, quite irrational, but the populace of Vienna convinced itself that the appearance of a male heir at this point would be a sign that their vicissitudes would shortly end. Thus, Joseph Benedict Augustus John Anthony Michael Adam of Hapsburg, born in the last hours of March 13, 1741, achieved his first triumph simply by being born a boy.[2] In Vienna placards were carried about, proclaiming that since the House of Hapsburg was once again dressed in trousers, Austria's enemies would speedily be put to flight. Popular rejoicing was general throughout the Empire.

The revelers greeting the birth of a prince with such glee did not merely seize a likely occasion to celebrate. They saw the dynasty strengthened, and in Austria the dynasty was paramount. It was possible in the eighteenth century, although barely, to conceive France without the Bourbons, and England had functioned quite acceptably during the Cromwellian interregnum, but Austria without the Hapsburgs was unthinkable. Being a congeries of diverse provinces, inhabited by Germans, Slavs, Magyars, Italians, and lesser nations, lacking a common language, cultural milieu or national economic interest, Austria was held together only by the dynasty. Making the most of whatever advantages their position as Holy Roman Emperors conferred on them, the Hapsburgs had assembled their vast but disparate dominions by taking full advantage of the political chaos occasioned by the intrusion of the Ottoman Turks into Southeastern Europe, and also by being undisputed masters at the game of diplomacy by marriage. Although their position as rulers of a great European power had been somewhat undermined by the outcome of the Thirty Years' War and their tacit abandonment of the claims to regulate the affairs of Germany, the power and the prestige retained by the Hapsburgs throughout the second half of the seventeenth century were still of imposing dimensions. Their position was particularly formidable in relation to the nobility in their various domains. The nobility in their lands might be arrogant, unruly, venal, grasping, rebellious, and disloyal, but all these qualities suffered from being parochial. Even in the larger national groupings the resources available to a dissident nobility were not on a scale available to the monarchy, which could, if necesary, draw upon a dozen or more such regions. In extreme cases it could take advantage of the circumstance that more often than not the nobles were separated from the oppressed peasantry not only by great differences in education, culture, and outlook, but frequently by language and nationality as well. Nor was it a case of all stick and no carrot. Even in the Thirty Years' War rewards for effective and loyal servants of the monarchy had been very substantial in terms of land grants in Bohemia and Moravia. Toward the end of the century the increasingly successful campaign waged by the Hapsburgs to dislodge the Turks from at least the northern Balkans had made further new territories available for distribution to those who had given proof of their trustworthiness.

The alienation of nobility from countryside, the erosion of its position in many provinces in the wake of various political disasters, the spoils to be had in Vienna, all combined to prevent the Austrian nobility from emerging as a viable political force, what in German is called *Geschichtsträger,* a class capable of identifying itself with conscious and defined political goals and of working toward their realization. The result was that the Hapsburgs, although their over-all resources werc far inferior to those, say, of the Bourbons, were able to exercise effective control over their dominions. The dynasty was the state. But in a sense it was *étatisme* without an *état.* England was undoubtedly an exceptional case, but in France the great authority of Versailles rested on a five-century-old tradition of expanding and carefully nurtured royal absolutism, allied with the practical interests of a not inconsiderable class deeply rooted in the provinces. There had been no corresponding pattern of development in Austria. The position of the monarchy was due more to arbitrary and often unrelated conditions; it was almost a case of unlimited authority *faute de mieux.* Such a situation might provide an unexcelled opportunity for an intelligent and purposeful ruler. It might also at any moment subside into an appallingly complete collapse.

Those who had expected a radical turn for the better with the birth of Joseph were to have their hopes dashed almost at once. Less than a month later Frederick II won a crushing victory over the Austrians at Mollwitz. Bavaria (which had never signed the Pragmatic Sanction), Saxony, and Spain entered the war against Austria and thus added to the already formidable coalition of France and Prussia. Anxious to muster whatever support she could, Maria Theresia journeyed to Pressburg in order to combine the ceremony of coronation with the Crown of St. Stephen with an appeal for help to the Hungarian Estates. The spectacle of a young and pretty queen in need of a gallant sword was irresistible to the Hungarian nobility; it responded with cries of *"Moriamur pro rege nostro"* but with hardly anything else. The story that the Queen appeared before them carrying the young

Archduke in her arms is untrue. At any rate, the monarchy was saved from dissolution, not because of the support of the Magyar Estates but rather because the opposing coalition was beset by more than the ordinary divisions to which coalitions were habitually susceptible. The French contented themselves with the dispatch of an auxiliary corps which under the incompetent leadership of Charles Albert of Bavaria was engaged for the most part in looting Upper Austria and Bohemia rather than in a full-scale attack upon Vienna. Meanwhile Frederick, unwilling to be the sponsor of Bavarian and Saxon aggrandizement, played his own game and concluded a separate peace at Kleinschnellendorf in November, when it appeared that Austria was about to be overwhelmed. Although he soon broke this agreement, the Austrians received the time they needed to concentrate their forces against the Bavarians. Thus, when in January 1742, Charles Albert had himself elected Holy Roman Emperor as Charles VII, Maria Theresia was able to repay this impertinence with the occupation of Munich in February. The following summer, at the urging of their unenthusiastic ally, Great Britain, the Austrians concluded peace. Silesia had to be ceded to Frederick, a loss to which Maria Theresia never reconciled herself, but she retained the balance of her dominions.

Archduke Joseph grew up in the Imperial Palace at Schönbrunn. Until he reached the age of seven, the boy was surrounded by women: his mother, his governess, the ladies of the court. His father seems to have indulged him in his rapidly developing stubbornness, without taking an active part in his education. Joseph systematically resisted all attempts to impose limits upon a native arrogance which must have been insufferable in a child of his age; he patronized the grandees of the realm, refused to seek forgiveness from those he had offended, and reacted against the feminine character of his surroundings by an outspoken preference for soldiers and military things. He flatly refused to learn anything. This promising career as an *enfant terrible* was blighted when, the Archduke having turned seven, Maria Theresia decided to take energetic measures to educate him. He was removed from the care of the ladies' circle, the Augustinian F. J. Weger was appointed as his tutor, and a separate Court was created for him. Field Marshal Count Karl Batthyany, in his capacity of *Ajo*, or guardian to Joseph, was selected by Maria Theresia to head the New Court. This gnarled old Magyar, veteran of the Turkish wars, has been much maligned. It has even been suggested that his rough manner was largely responsible for brutalizing a sensitive soul, for turning the young prince for all time into someone who despised his fellow men. Joseph is said to have remarked later that the only thing he learned from Batthyany was the lapidary phrase which Goethe, by putting it into Goetz von Berlichingen's mouth, was to endow with a classical respectability. But the old soldier was meant, after all, to make the boy a little more amenable to discipline. The Empress was explicit about this in her instructions to him: All flatterers were to be removed from the Archduke's surroundings, he was to be broken of the habit of criticizing everyone at the least provocation, and above all, he was to learn self-discipline. Batthyany simply proceeded to treat Joseph as he would any refractory subaltern; the assumption that a boy being trained to become a soldier would be broken in spirit by being growled at by an old hero seems highly gratuitous.

More baneful, undoubtedly, was Batthyany's influence over the selection of the tutors who were to supervise the way the Archduke used his time. With the exception of the already mentioned Weger, they seem to have been hopeless pedants. Joseph, as was to be sure the case with most of his contemporaries, was put to memorizing endless, and to him meaningless, passages on a variety of subjects, one duller than the other. The worst offender was surely old Johann Christoph von Bartenstein, who, from Joseph's tenth year on, replaced Weger as his principal teacher of history. While Weger had concentrated his efforts upon encouraging the Archduke to learn about the heroes and great deeds of old, perhaps a reasonable method when dealing with a child of that age, Bartenstein went about his task more systematically. Joseph was to learn in detail at least the history of his future dominions. In Bartenstein's opinion there were no satisfactory materials in existence for this purpose, and he consequently decided to write these himself. He had the necessary leisure for this as he had previously, by his impossible manner, made himself so unpopular in his official capacity as *Staatssekretär* that people went to almost any lengths to avoid having to enter his office. He eventually produced a gigantic work which ran to fourteen volumes of text and six of appendices, although it did not go beyond the reign of Rudolf II (d. 1612). Unfortunately, it is quite unreadable even for professional historians. What a child of ten or twelve must have made of it defies the imagination. Joseph did not grow up with much love for history, although it would certainly be an exaggeration to maintain that his later determination to break with the past in so many ways was a reaction to Bartenstein's methods.

History seems to have occupied the central place in Joseph's

education. As the principal court chamberlain, Prince Khevenhüller, observed, the intention was to accomplish the same goal
through history that the author of "that excellent work entitled
"Télémaque" had achieved through the means of fable. But this
did not mean that the Archduke was not exposed to the whole
gamut of academic learning. We know that he was also given les-
sons in mathematics, geography, Latin, literary history, biblical
studies, and modern languages, and was subjected to frequent
and public examinations in all of them. He seems to have ex-
celled only in mathematics and languages, achieving a tolerable
fluency in French, Italian, and Czech while still in his early teens.
When he did rather less well than was expected of him in his
other subjects Bartenstein remarked to Maria Theresia that evidently there were only three means of achieving results in education: punishment, reward, and competition. Given the Archduke's peculiar nature he would hesitate long before advising
against the complete omission of the first of these. Nothing could
be worse than to show any sign of softness toward him. On the
other hand, most of what could be achieved by punishment could
just as easily be brought about by the promise of an appropriate
reward. All things considered, it would be best to stimulate the
reluctant scholar by putting at his side an apt young fellow from
the *Theresianum* who would shame him into working harder.
This stratagem was actually adopted for a time, but unfortunately we know nothing of how well it worked or of young Joseph's relationship with his no doubt somewhat awed fellow
pupil.[3]

Maria Theresia, pious almost to a fault, saw to it that Joseph's
religious education was not neglected. Besides requiring him to
attend a daily mass, morning and evening prayers, and daily ves-
pers, she provided him with formal instruction in the tenets of
Catholicism three times a week. Over and above this came his
obligations and feast days and religious holy days. For instance, it
is reported that during Easter week of 1752 the eleven-year-old
Archduke attended services in no less than eighteen Viennese
churches. It is perhaps surprising that this regimen did not succeed in turning Joseph into a religious obsessive, nor did it elicit
from him a violent reaction against religion; but the fact is that
throughout his life, although he remained always a convinced
and orthodox Catholic, his religion for the most part sat fairly
easily on him.

Although the reports dealing with Joseph's continuing education tend to confine themselves to generalities which do not really

permit a definitive judgment about the bulk of his reading matter, and much less about what works really had much influence on him, it seems that in his fourteenth year he began for the first time to take a serious interest in his studies. The subject which ultimately came to fascinate him was the then relatively new one of *Naturrecht,* which can perhaps best be translated as political economy. This discipline concerned itself in a systematic way with the question of how realms would be most rationally and effectively governed. Many of its fundamental assumptions were derived from the school of French physiocrats which was then at the height of its intellectual fashion. Its chief advocate and ornament in Vienna was Karl Anton von Martini.

It has frequently been alleged, but never established, that Martini himself taught Joseph. What is certain is that one of Martini's disciples, Christian August Beck, functioned in the capacity of Bartenstein's assistant. Not to be outdone by his chief, Beck also drew up a massive compendium for the guidance of the Archduke. It eventually came to well over a thousand folio pages. Its resemblance to Bartenstein's monstrous compilation ended there, however. Beck had initially been instructed, probably by Bartenstein, to produce an abstract of a work entitled *De Officio Hominis et Civis* by the seventeenth-century legal philosopher Samuel Pufendorf. Beck had expanded his labors by including annotated selections from such diverse writers on politics as Frederick II of Prussia and Montesquieu. The work struck a nice balance between protestations of belief in the unchallengeable authority of the absolute ruler and reminders that his authority was subject to a higher one: significantly, not only the authority of the Almighty, but also a ruler's duty to keep in mind the welfare of the State and the happiness of his subjects. No more explicit blueprint for what had already come to be called "enlightened despotism" has ever been produced, and there is good reason to believe that Joseph read it conscientiously.

As he grew into young manhood, Joseph was turning into something of a recluse. The child who had been so hard to educate was to grow up to be a man who concerned himself only with weighty matters. Although he had been made to learn to play the 'cello, he had no talent for music. Nor did he hunt. Describing the chase as an egregious waste of time, he refused to join in it even when his absence was a clear breach of court etiquette. He never troubled to even learn the rules of the card games of which his mother was so fond. He did not like to dance. He avoided as much as possible the company of his by now numerous brothers and sisters, describing them not very tactfully as so many useless ornaments which had to be maintained at great expense to the state. His famous friendship with his brother Leopold did not develop until the latter had left Vienna and had been installed in Milan as Grand Duke of Tuscany. Nor did Joseph get on well with his father. It is undoubtedly an exaggeration to say that he held Francis Stephen, who in the meantime had been elected Emperor, in contempt because he allowed his wife to rule him completely and to exclude him from the affairs of State, but there is ample evidence that Joseph thought his father led an empty and unproductive life. As has already been noted, Joseph detested hunting, an activity which Francis Stephen engaged in rather to excess, and he did not have the breadth of vision to see that the Emperor's other passion, the expansion of the family fortune, went considerably beyond the mere amassing of money. Joseph never really understood that by introducing more rational and efficient western methods into the concerns he had himself invested in, his father had been one of the most important architects of the somewhat belated industrialization of the Austrian lands. At any rate, the Archduke cut himself off from the usual pleasures and pursuits of adolescents. Increasingly, all the energies which in a young man of his years might justifiably have been dissipated in frivolity, were in him channeled into introspection and brooding about his position and the duties he would one day have to assume.[4]

When Joseph was twenty he for the first time gave vent to the thoughts resulting from his broodings. He submitted a memorandum to the Empress in which he addressed himself to what appeared to him the most pressing questions of the moment.[5] If nothing else, the breadth of his purview commands attention. In the space of no more than a dozen pages, he ranges from foreign policy to internal administration to the organization of the army. Hard upon a suggestion to divide the country into military districts in order to facilitate its defense came another to breed all the mares in the cavalry. The document is evidently a shot-gun proposal advanced by a young enthusiast who has not yet learned to discriminate between the essential and the tertiary. But there is in the memorandum the unmistakable voice of the reformer. Joseph not only insists that the state must be run more efficiently, that extravagance and needless expenditure must be avoided, sinecures cut off, and salaries of high officials reduced to more reasonable levels, but he proposes that in order to finance the military reorganization which he regarded as essential, the Austrian nobility give up its cherished immunity from direct taxation.

If Joseph's measures had been adopted at once and in their entirety, there is little doubt that the state would have collapsed. But there was no danger of this. Maria Theresia seems not even to have dignified Joseph's effusions with an answer. Joseph himself subsequently recognized the impractical character of the document and referred to it as his *Träumereien,* youthful dreams.

By this time the young dreamer was married. He had grown into a very presentable young man of average height and slim figure, his best feature being his incredibly blue eyes, so blue that a new color purporting to reproduce their particular shade became the rage of Viennese fashion. As was only to be expected, the young ladies of the court, encouraged no doubt by their mothers, ran after him shamelessly. But the Archduke was apparently immune to all their charms. One disappointed beauty had the wit to remark that he was as cold as that other Joseph of Egypt. Nor, as so often was the case with highly moral young princes, did he fall hopelessly in love with some no doubt lovely but quite unsuitable princess. Rather, he regarded himself as the most natural instrument of dynastic policy, and did not for a moment question Maria Theresia's right to arrange for him whatever marriage appeared most desirable in the light of the current political situation. Heirs to great thrones married early as a rule, and Joseph's apparent antipathy to women only reinforced Maria Theresia's intention to marry him off early. The wife she chose for him was the eighteen-year-old Princess Isabella of Bourbon-Parma, a granddaughter of Louis XV. The match would have the two-fold advantage of enhancing Austrian influence in Italy and of serving to reinforce the recent alliance with France of which the Empress still expected great things. The two young people were married in Vienna in October 1760, with a pomp and splendor that quite belied the fact that Austria was engaged once again in a great war. Isabella was not only a beautiful young girl but a highly intelligent and well-educated young woman as well. Joseph almost at once fell desperately in love with his wife. The next few years were to be the only happy ones of his life.[6] They would also see the emergence of a relationship which would be a determining one in Joseph's career. It was during this period that he began to fall under the spell of Prince Kaunitz.

CHAPTER II

Archduke and King of the Romans

PRINCE WENZEL ANTON KAUNITZ HAD A REPUTATION AS AN ECCEN-
tric in a century in which uncommon behavior attracted far less
attention than is the case today. He was so inordinately vain that
it was reported that in order to be sure of having an evenly pow-
dered wig, he would make his servants stir up a bag of powder
with fans and would then walk about the room stark naked so
that the powder would descend on him. He always carried with
him an elaborate set of instruments intended for the cleaning of
his teeth and would bring these into play at dinner with appropriate rinsing and spitting noises, no matter how formal the set-
ting. He had a mortal fear of drafts and the night air, and for this
reason would in no circumstances quit his bed before noon. His
aversion to death was so pronounced that it was not even permissible, in his presence, to allude to someone being in ill health.
Once he sent birthday greetings and a cake to an aunt who had
died several years before, and no one had the courage to tell
him that these were no longer required. If he was frustrated in
the smallest matter, he at once took to his bed and refused to
arise, sometimes for weeks on end.

Born in 1711, the son of an ultra-Catholic Bohemian noble
family, he was nevertheless, for unknown reasons, sent to study at
the Protestant university at Leipzig. This institution enjoyed at
that time the reputation of being the foremost German center for
legal studies. Both its faculty and curriculum had been considerably influenced by the views of the recently deceased legal philosopher Christian Thomasius, views which were empirical, eclectic,
and liberal. It is uncertain, however, to what extent the young
Kaunitz partook of them, as he only spent one academic year in
Leipzig. In the fall of 1732 he was sent on the grand tour which
was a necessary part of the education of every young nobleman of
means.

His journey lasted for something less than a year; it was shorter
than customary, probably because his family lacked the funds to
support him in idleness any longer. But during this abbreviated

Bildungsreise he reached a crucial decision. At considerable expense his family had secured for him a canonry in Münster, in Westphalia. It was intended that he should ultimately become a bishop there. Now he renounced this benefice. There are no indications about what considerations moved him to come to this decision. Perhaps merely a horror of dank and parochial Westphalia. At any rate, young Kaunitz in 1735 took the oath of office and became a member of the *Reichshofrat*. At first he was occupied with the usual insignificant details of internal administration that were the lot of the junior clerk, but in the swollen organism which was responsible for the conduct of foreign affairs as well, he succeeded somehow in drawing attention to himself as a potential diplomatic talent. As has been noted, as early as 1740 he was offered an important diplomatic post, that of Minister to Denmark, which he turned down. His excuse was that his health could not stand the rigorous climate of Copenhagen, an argument which was at least plausible. His refusal did not harm his career. In 1741 he was sent to Italy to bring official notice of the birth of a crown prince. In this way his association with Joseph began.

Kaunitz' advancement was rapid. He filled the important post of Minister to Turin and then that of High Chamberlain to the Archduchess Maria Anna in Brussels. In this latter capacity he was in fact chiefly responsible for defending the Austrian Netherlands against the attacks of the French. The isolated position of these provinces and the impossibility of retaining them against really determined French opposition did not escape him. At the conclusion of the war he played a leading role in the negotiations that led to the Peace of Aix-la-Chapelle. In 1750 he was appointed to the top diplomatic post in the Austrian service, that of Minister to France. There are indications that already then he had decided that Austrian policy had reached an impasse. It was quite evident that the overriding constant for Vienna was the enmity of Prussia, and the relations of the two countries had just been drastically exacerbated by the loss of Silesia to Frederick. The traditional alliance with England was not likely to produce a combination strong enough to defeat both Prussia and France. Perhaps it was time to bury the traditional rivalry of Hapsburg and Valois. These thoughts were certainly being entertained by Kaunitz some years before the tumultuous appearance of the Russian Empire on the European diplomatic scene led to the great reversal of alliances. What is clear is that from the first Kaunitz employed his talents in Paris to achieve much better relations with France. In 1753 he was appointed *Staatskanzler*, a position which came as close to that of First Minister as the ponderous administrative machinery of the Hapsburg realms allowed. Henceforth his views and foreign policy would no longer be merely those of an isolated, if highly regarded, diplomat, but those of the official responsible for the formulation of policy.[1]

In 1754 the perennial brushes between British and French patrols in North America began once more to take on a threatening nature. Soon the two powers were again at war. Great Britain, under the terms of its old alliance with Austria, asked for help. Kaunitz, without actually giving a categorical refusal, hung back. The British, justifiably miffed, began to make overtures in the direction of Prussia, which in January 1756 led to the conclusion of the Convention of Westminster between these two powers. This played into Kaunitz' hands. In May of the same year he was able to conclude a defensive alliance with France, thus completing the celebrated Diplomatic Revolution. As Austria for some years had had a similar arrangement with Russia it appeared that at long last Frederick would be faced with insuperable odds. Nevertheless, the King of Prussia, informed of Austrian military preparations through the treasonous conduct of an official, decided to take the offensive at once. He started operations with an attack upon Saxony and succeeded in knocking the Saxons out of the war before the Austrians could lend them any effective help. The course of the Seven Years' War is too well known to require a narration here. Suffice it to say that in spite of some striking victories won by the reorganized Austrian armies, under Field Marshal Laudon in particular (Kunersdorf, Landshut), the difficulties of working in conjunction with the Russians who, far from their homeland, were operating very cautiously, and the circumstance that the French were heavily engaged against England in the colonies vitiated the advantage the Austrians might otherwise have had. The succession of the deranged Peter III to the Russian throne in 1762 led to a Russian withdrawal from the war, and as there was now patently no further chance of defeating Frederick, peace was concluded with the Prussians at Hubertusburg in 1763. To the intense mortification of Maria Theresia and Kaunitz, Frederick was left in possession of Silesia.

While Austria engaged in this long and futile struggle, Joseph was getting his introduction to the serious work of governing. In 1761 Maria Theresia decreed that henceforth he should attend the meetings of the *Staatsrath*. It can not be maintained that he attained much distinction in the capacity of observer. The role did not suit his temperament. His mocking remark that he expected to find himself among Solons and Lycurguses but instead was forced to sit through endless formal exercises in rhetoric, is an undeserved stricture on Austria's statesmen. Kaunitz, in particular, was entirely capable of addressing himself to the point if he wished. It seems clear enough that the members of the *Staatsrath,* who were after all responsible to the Empress alone, preferred, in Joseph's presence, to take refuge in safe generalities, particularly as they were by no means unaware of his fire-eating tendencies. At any rate, the Archduke was effectively excluded from any substantive discussions. It did not take long for him to become embittered and to turn to other pursuits.[2]

Characteristically, Joseph did not compensate for his lack of a meaningful political occupation by devoting himself, as his father had done before him, to any one of the usual pleasures of princes. Instead, he seemed to take an almost perverse pleasure in playing the part of an obedient, submissive servant of his mother. He ran little errands for her, such as going to Maria Zell, which was being developed into a place for public pilgrimages. This mission greatly pleased the pious Maria Theresia, all the more when Joseph protested that even such a brief absences from her were to him intolerable.[3] It would be amiss to read a hypocritical tone into these protestations. His self-abusement was sincere. Also, he at this time threw himself into the part of a dutiful model husband.

In this latter endeavor, at least, Joseph did not have to dissemble. Not only was he very much in love with Isabella, but he recognized without jealousy that she was easily his intellectual equal. She was interested not only in works of pious contemplation, as would not have been unusual for a person in her position, but also in moral philosophy and even history. She composed a little work on Prussia which is full of the most incisive observations about the true nature of that ambitious state. Armed with the most precise instructions from the Court of Parma about what attitude to adopt vis-à-vis the leading personalities of the Court of Vienna, she soon improved upon these as the result of experience. She captivated everybody. Maria Theresia loved her without reservation, and Joseph easily fell into the habit of thinking of himself as her slave.

Unfortunately, Isabella was anything but the dream princess the court imagined her to be. Her nature was, in fact, hopelessly complex. After her marriage she was occupied increasingly with the most morbid speculations. Whether this was because a gypsy had at one time prophesied that she would die early or for deeper psychological reasons it is impossible to tell, but she came not only to concentrate upon thoughts of death in the most unhealthy way, but even to desire her own early demise with what amounted to fierce passion. Worse, she did not love her husband. She was, so far as one knows, at all times amiable and compliant, but the emotion of love she reserved for his sister Maria Christina, Mimi. Her protestations in her letters of the deepest attachment to Mimi are so intense that one is really tempted to speculate about the relationship of what seemed to border on forbidden emotions and her all but suicidal tendencies. The notion of a great guilt, to be propitiated, at all costs, certainly suggests itself.[4]

Joseph certainly suffered because of his wife's spiritual crises, which so far as we know manifested themselves in a steadily more withdrawn demeanor. His reaction to this was identical to that which he displayed toward his mother. Maria Theresia arbitrarily excluded him from the real business of government; he would repay her by becoming the very model of an obedient son. Isabella was cold to him; he would be an even more perfect husband. In all probability the real depth of his wife's melancholy remained hidden from him.

So, at least on the surface, this was a happy time for the Archduke. He spent every moment he could glean from his official duties in the company of his wife. In 1762 a daughter whom they named Maria Theresia was born to them, and Joseph fell easily into the role of the doting father. He and his wife entertained at musical soirées, at which she played the violin and he the piano. But these scenes of domestic bliss were only too brief. Motherhood merely served to heighten Isabella's despair. On New Year's day 1763 she wrote to Mimi and mentioned almost casually that she did not expect to live through the year. In July she became ill, but then recovered. Soon afterward she was again pregnant. Then, in November, she suddenly became ill with smallpox. The Court physician, the Dutchman Van Swieten who enjoyed the Empress' unshakable confidence, was summoned. He undertook to bleed the Archduchess, but with predictably negative results. Isabella, although only in her sixth month, gave birth to a daughter who lived only two hours. On the 27th she died. Joseph was crushed. His letters to his father-in-law, the Duke of Parma, give proof of far more than conventional grief. There is a story to the effect that his grief was so great that Mimi, in order to recall him to this life, revealed to him his wife's real coldness toward him, but this seems unlikely.[5] It is perfectly true that henceforth Joseph always kept women at arm's length. Still, he did not feel that he had been betrayed by Isabella, but rather by fate. He would not give it a hostage again.

The past few years had thus seen Joseph largely taken up with his personal affairs. He also worked long hours, to be sure, but mostly at petty tasks which did not for the most part engage his intellect. It is, for instance, possible to read all of his correspondence in this period without actually becoming aware that Austria was in the midst of a great war. But he was not allowed to give himself over to his private grief. Reasons of state demanded that he begin to play a more public part in the affairs of the realm.

For Maria Theresia and Kaunitz perhaps the most distressing aspect of the unsuccessful struggle against Prussian ambition, which had now lasted almost a quarter of a century, had been the brief period during which even the Imperial crown had been lost to the House of Hapsburg. The Imperial dignity might be largely an empty one, but it had been in the family for so long that, at least in their eyes, it had assumed an importance far out of proportion to its real worth. They did not want to lose it again. In order to guard against any further unpleasant surprises, Joseph was to be crowned King of the Romans in his father's lifetime. This title, which originally had been the really operant one, that of Holy Roman Emperor representing merely a gilding of an already resplendent lily by papal action, had later on been debased into nothing more than the usual designation for the heir apparent to the Imperial throne. But even so, it was necessary to be chosen King of the Romans by the Electors before one could so style oneself. And the most influential of the Electors was no less a person than Frederick the Great. Ordinarily he might have been expected to do everything in his power to oppose an action guaranteeing that the Imperial dignity would remain with the Hapsburgs. But the times were not ordinary. The Prussian king had been brought to the edge of irremediable disaster in the later stages of the Seven Years' War and although he had been saved by the accession of Peter III, he seems to have been considerably sobered by the experience. It was, for the time being, his intention to live in peace with his German neighbors. He could not, at any rate, oppose them over the matter of the Imperial succession. Accordingly, a clause was incorporated into the Peace of Hubertusburg, which ended the war between Austria and Prussia, wherein Frederick promised to give his vote to the Hapsburg candidate. There being now no serious opposition, arrangements were made for Joseph's election in Frankfurt in March 1764.[6]

The election and subsequent coronation were accompanied by the traditional medieval pomp of the Empire. The Imperial party traveling to Frankfurt was a brilliant one. Aside from Joseph it included many of the highest dignitaries of the Austrian court and was headed by Emperor Francis Stephen himself. There was a ceremonial entry by the party in their richly decorated but antiquated, uncomfortable and quite unsafe state coaches. Joseph, dressed in the heavily embroidered coronation costume, felt weighed down, ill at ease, even ridiculous. The election which followed was a formality and on the third day of April Joseph was crowned. Goethe, who was then fifteen and witnessed the ceremony, describes it in *Dichtung und Wahrheit:* "The coronation robes were much too large for the new King of the Romans who rather gave the impression of being at a masquerade ball; the crown of Charlemagne had had to be stuffed with large quantities of cotton so that it should fit his head at all; from time to time, in excuse for his peculiar appearance, he would smile self-deprecatingly at his father." [7] Later on there would be those who maintained that Joseph's behavior during the ceremonies was a deliberate and conscious rejection of old institutions, inspired by his reforming ideas.[8] There is little evidence to support this. The mood which pervades his letters to Maria Theresia written from Frankfurt vacillates between bitterness at having to participate in such gaudy ceremonies at a time when he could think of very little but his dead wife and self-mockery for cutting such a ridiculous figure. But it is clear that he is making fun of himself, not of the dignity which he assumed in however undignified a manner.

Throughout these undoubtedly trying days, Joseph also had something else on his mind. Isabella had not been dead three months when Kaunitz began to insist that for reasons of state Joseph would have to marry as soon as practicable. At first Joseph rejected the notion out of hand. He intended to remain a widower all his life. When his mother insisted, his answer was that he could envisage only being married to a woman with the heart, the manner, the spirit, the eyes, the teeth, the figure, the bosom of his late wife. As it happens, he was not merely putting Maria Theresia off, but actually had someone in mind: Louise of Parma, Isabella's sister, then fourteen years old. She was said to bear an uncanny resemblance to her sister, and the fact that the marriage, because of her age, would have to be postponed for a year or two was from Joseph's point of view, a distinct advantage. The match would have fallen well within the prohibited degrees, and the Empress was averse to it for this reason; but she as well as he knew that she could easily get a dispensation for her son. Accordingly, the Duke of Parma was once more approached on Joseph's behalf.⁹ He had nothing against the union, he had grown fond of his son-in-law who corresponded with him regularly, but unfortunately there was a previous commitment. Louise had been promised to the Bourbon prince of Spain. The Spanish Court, approached about the possibility of withdrawing its claim, proved obdurate and Kaunitz was unwilling to endanger the precious French alliance by insisting. Thus the matter had to be dropped.

It happened that there was a momentary dearth of available Catholic princesses of sufficiently high station. There were, as a matter of fact, only three others who could be considered at all eligible: the princesses of Portugal, Saxony, and Bavaria. Having already suffered what he was bound to regard as a diminution of his international bargaining position by his approaches to Spain because of Joseph's desire to marry his late wife's sister, Kaunitz was not in the mood to consult the prospective bridegroom about his preferences. The matter would be decided solely on dynastic grounds. The Infanta of Portugal, who at least had the advantage of being beautiful, was eliminated because the Chancellor was of the opinion that England was so entrenched in Portugal that not even a royal marriage could shake her position there. Thus there was nothing to be gained in that direction. As there was not much to choose between the advantages of extending Austrian influence over Saxony or Bavaria, Joseph was to be allowed a choice between these two princesses. A meeting with Kunigunde of Saxony was arranged, but she proved to be so ferociously ugly as to elicit from Joseph a series of remarks which made Maria Theresia hastily shift the attack to Maria Josefa of Bavaria. Alas, this lady was not much more attractive. Her intended husband described her as being short, fat, not youthful in appearance (she was three years older than he), with pimples and ugly red spots on her face, and ugly teeth. It was less than love at first sight. But Kaunitz alluded forcibly to the great advantages to be gained in Bavaria, more particularly since the Bavarian branch of the House of Wittelsbach seemed to be heading for extinction in the not too distant future, and Joseph bowed reluctantly to *raison d'état*. In view of the circumstances of this marriage it is astonishing that the direct political advantages which accrued to the House of Hapsburg as its result were more than modest. What is anything but astonishing is that the marriage, which took place at Schönbrunn in January 1765, turned out to be an almost comi-

cally bad one. Joseph told his mother, his sister, almost anyone he
spoke with, that he could not abide his wife. He demonstratively
did not share her bed, avoided her on all occasions, even had a
high partition put up between their respective balconies so that
he would not have to gaze upon her when he took the sun for a
few minutes. The poor woman wept openly, complained to all
who would listen, and succeeded in making herself thoroughly
ridiculous.[10]

While Joseph was thus successfully avoiding the delights of a
married state he did not wish to be in, his whole situation suddenly and dramatically changed. As already noted, Joseph's relations with his father were ambivalent. He was fond of him, he
never lacked in filial respect, but he entertained sharply censor-
ious opinions about Francis Stephen's mode of life, which in his
view bordered on the useless. Francis Stephen was Emperor, to be
sure, but so long as he acquiesced in being nothing more than
prince consort to Maria Theresia, the Imperial dignity amounted
to very little. This, of course, suited Maria Theresia perfectly. She
felt herself to be solely responsible for conducting the business of
her house which had ruled in Austria for almost half a millen-
nium, and she did not wish to share her power with anyone. It
was, perhaps, a pity that Maria Theresia excluded her husband so
vigorously from all political responsibility, as he was in reality a
very able man. He had been given his first and only official task
early in their marriage when he had been put in command of
part of the Austrian forces facing the Prussians, but military talent was something which he lacked to an imposing degree. After
the resultant fiasco, the Empress concluded somewhat too rapidly
that her husband's abilities lay exclusively in the private sphere
and kept him completely away from the work of government.[11]
That this was a mistake is shown by the model administration
that he enforced on the province of Tuscany, which he had received in exchange for his beloved Lorraine at the time of their
marriage. Tuscany, maladministered for centuries and only recently acquired by the Hapsburgs, emerged under him as their
richest possession. Be that as it may, he made no attempt whatever to interfere in the work of governing elsewhere. But, of
course, this arrangement was due largely to his complacency.

CHAPTER III

The Emperor

IN 1765 MARIA THERESIA AND KAUNITZ AGREED BETWEEN THEM
that the interests of the House of Hapsburg would best be served
if Tuscany were to remain in a somewhat set-apart position, as a
kind of *secundo-genitur*. Thus it should not go to Joseph, who
would inherit everything else one day, but to the next oldest
prince, his brother Leopold. Accordingly, Francis Stephen added
an appropriate codicil to his will, and Joseph in a public ceremony renounced his rights to it for all time. The renunciation
displeased him, but once again he played the obedient son. It
happened that these events took place just prior to Leopold's marriage to the Spanish Infanta Marie Louise. As Leopold was going
to Tuscany anyway, it was decided to celebrate the nuptials in
Innsbruck, which would be on his route, and the Court thus
made its way to Tyrol. The wedding took place on the fifth of
August. The Court stayed on and on August 18 attended an Italian play. The Emperor left the performance early. He was not
feeling too well and had been subject to spells of dizziness for
some time. As he was making for his rooms, followed at a few
paces by Joseph, he suddenly stopped and leaned for support
against the wall of a narrow corridor. Joseph ran to him and
urged him to sit down. The Emperor replied that it was nothing,
just one of his dizzy spells. But as soon as, supported by his son,
he reached his apartments, he collapsed onto a couch. A physician
was summoned at once; he arrived within a few minutes and immediately bled the Emperor from arm and temple. But it was too
late. It had been a massive stroke, and Francis Stephen died
within another minute or two, cradled in the arms of Joseph.[1]

Maria Theresia, who had been informed at once, fell into a
complete collapse. She spent the whole night keening and only
toward morning felt the relief of tears. At first she would see no
one but the members of her family and seemed completely
stunned. As a sign of her widowhood she caused her beautiful
long hair to be cut off, and she never again appeared in public
except in black. She was not so prostrate, however, as to forget to

dictate long and detailed instructions to Leopold before his departure for Florence.² Upon her own return to Vienna she once more seems to have given way to her grief and spoke of retiring to a convent and turning over the government to Joseph. But Kaunitz dissuaded her from this. It has been suggested that he feared that Joseph, who had already given some indication of his independence of mind, would soon dispense with his services and that he realized that he could retain his position only if the Empress stayed on. Such calculations may well have played a part in determining the nature of the advice he gave Maria Theresia, but there is no real evidence that they did. However this may have been, Maria Theresia soon overcame her depression sufficiently to convince herself that her peoples still needed her and that she could not shirk her duty to them.

Still, something had to be done with Joseph. Having previously been elected King of the Romans, he automatically became Emperor upon the death of his father. He would now have to be associated in a more direct manner with the inner workings of government. Both the Empress and Kaunitz realized that the new Emperor's temperament differed radically from his father's and that, somehow, employment would have to be found for him. As, however, Maria Theresia was not, after all, resigning her powers, the exact nature of what this was to be presented some difficulty. And, as this was Austria, first of all a formula would have to be found. The substance would follow.

Again, in all probability acting upon a suggestion from Kaunitz, Maria Theresia, immediately following upon her return to Vienna, designated Joseph to be Grand Master of the Orders of Maria Theresia and St. Stephen with the title of Co-Regent. The heads of all administrative departments took an oath of allegiance to him in this last capacity. What the significance of this new title was in practical terms was anybody's guess, but one could glean a hint from the official announcement of these steps, in which was incorporated a sentence to the effect that the Empress had no intention whatever of allowing the new arrangements to alienate any of her authority over the indivisible lands of the Austrian Crown. In spite of this conservative tone which should have inclined him to caution, Joseph, genuinely saddened as he was about the death of his father, could not at the same time suppress a certain note of elation. It was certainly true that Maria Theresia had given every indication that she proposed to withdraw at least to a considerable extent from the direction of affairs and it seemed to him that his hour had at long last struck.

At last he would be able to begin with the implementation of some of the changes he had been turning over in his mind for the last few years.[3]

It would not be psychologically correct to maintain, as is often done, that Joseph, as soon as he had reason to believe that he had the power to influence the course of affairs, ran away with the bit in his teeth. Impetuosity was never one of his faults. After all, he had for years made no secret of what he intended to do once he had the power to act; he had explained his intentions at length to his immediate entourage, and he is not to be blamed for failing to realize that his ideas had gained neither general currency nor wholehearted acceptance. That would have taken much more experience than he possessed at the time. He went wrong, rather, in 1765 in two different ways, both of which would continue to characterize his reign to such a degree that it is difficult to refrain from thinking of them as congenital limitations. First, he proposed a practical reform which, although rational and promising, was so complicated and exotic that even those who would benefit were not convinced of its advantages. Secondly, he asked for a program of reform so sweeping and complex that while the individual proposals might all be praiseworthy and consistent with the existing system, the impression it gave was one of revolutionary upheaval. Or, at least this could be plausibly asserted by those who had reason to fear any given change. In Joseph, this represented more than merely tactical miscalculation. It was the emanation of a spirit which was already then both pedantic and doctrinaire.

Joseph's first mistake in 1765 concerned the late Emperor's inheritance, which had gone to him in its entirety. It was a goodly sum, no less than 22 million florins. As this money represented Francis Stephen's private fortune, greatly increased by sagacious investments, no one could have made the least objection if Joseph had chosen to add it to his own privy purse. Instead, he decided to turn it over to the State. As he had a deep-seated aversion to waste, and was convinced that the expenses of the Court were ruinous, although in comparison to those of France they were quite modest, he gave the money for the purpose of retiring a part of the national debt. The impact of the gift was such that the interest paid by the Crown, which had risen to nearly six percent yearly, now dropped to four. It was estimated that this represented a saving of some 870,000 florins annually.[4] This was a considerable advantage, but the effect upon the individual was indirect and the economic climate of Austria was by no means so advanced that the availability of cheap money created, as it would have in a more modern state, at least a modest wave of prosperity. The average man merely grumbled that his taxes were as high as they had ever been.

The Emperor's second major mistake in 1765 was a repetition of an earlier one. As we have already observed, he had some years before submitted the *Träumereien* to his mother, and succeeded only in thoroughly frightening her and her advisers. He had himself come to realize the impracticality of those youthful suggestions. He now sent her another memorandum, much longer, better thought out, more in keeping with what was possible, but no less ambitious and uncompromising. As this document not only gives a fairly complete insight into the Emperor's state of mind at the time of his accession, but also incorporates much of what was to become his lifework, we must now examine it in some detail.[5]

Joseph began by dismissing as useless both those who ran heedlessly after everything new or different and those who followed blindly in the tracks of their predecessors. He intended to follow neither of these extremes. He realized that he still lacked a measure of experience, but he had already seen and learned enough to deliver himself of some opinions. To begin with, the finances of the realm needed reform very badly. Here he would refuse to be guided by this or that fashionable doctrine. He had already seen enough of the harm that such Procrustean systems did. In matters of finance he intended to be an atheist; empiricism would have to prevail. But in the mechanics of bringing about these changes, he could discern a number of fixed rules. To begin with, the administrative personnel of the Monarchy would have to undergo a major overhaul. With the one exception of Kaunitz not a single minister had rendered any worthwhile service to the State for some years. Whatever had been accomplished had been the work of twelve men, *i.e.* the *Staatsrath*. Inevitably this system resulted in two or more opinions being presented on every question, and the monarch often had no way to choose between proposals coming to him from different groups of trusted advisers, but contradictory in nature. It would be much better to refer a question to one man only. (Here, be it noted, is the germ of the Emperor's favorite administrative procedure adopted later on.)

Another great failing of the Austrian administration, as the Emperor saw it, was the unwillingness of department heads to delegate authority or to trust their subordinates. They bombarded them with questions about every stage of a project they had reluctantly turned over to them and the resulting *Papier-krieg* would end up by costing vastly more money than it was intended to save. In order to introduce a more rational tone into the administration it would be necessary, first, to redefine the spheres of responsibility of the various departments. In this way everyone would have a clearly defined task and would be able to concentrate on the substance rather than on the form of his job. Every year, two commandants, one civilian, one military, should be appointed in every province of the Empire, and theirs alone would be the responsibility for one calendar year. In Vienna, the chiefs of the eight ministries should enjoy a like independence, but their dates of appointment should be staggered at monthly intervals so that their reports would not all be due at the same time and thus create a hopeless confusion of contradictory opinions. It is not difficult to imagine how such a farrago of overly simplistic analysis, naive and antiquated solutions, and radical suggestions must have been greeted by those into whose sphere it fell. But there was a great deal more to come.

Having unburdened himself of his opinion on what he considered the most pressing questions, Joseph proceeded to add, more or less at random, observations on some of the other shortcomings of the Monarchy: a) Education was grossly neglected, particularly among people of good family who regarded it as little more than a process which inculcated the social graces and a modicum of piety. At any rate, those who benefited from this exiguous system lacked seriousness and had no higher ambition than to run after all the only too available amusements of Vienna; it would be much better to place institutions of higher education in provincial cities, as was the case in Germany, so that the students would not forever be distracted. Also, the professors were paid far too well; this enabled them to subsist without having to give private tutorial sessions, and this led to a neglect of the students. b) Those young men of noble birth who chose not to attend a university should not be permitted to sink without trace into a life of idleness but should be required to perform at least three years of military service as unpaid volunteers. c) All persons actively engaged in State service, and their wives, should have preference at Court over even members of the most ancient houses if these were not engaged in serving the State. d) To make more people available for State service, no one was to be permitted to take holy orders before the age of twenty-five, however much the Pope and all the monks in the universe might protest. e) All monastic foundations were to be examined by an impartial commission; those found wanting were to be either reformed or secularized. f) The police force was to be reformed under a competent chief; it would be well to make use of men invalided out of the army for police duty. g) All departments should do their utmost to employ wounded veterans or those drawing pensions, as this would permit the curtailment of these charges to the State. h) For obvious economic reasons, the State should do everything possible to attract foreigners to spend their money there; this would become very difficult as long as foreign visitors were subjected to harassment because they happened to subscribe to different religious opinions and their books were confiscated as they crossed the frontiers; while it is certainly the duty of a monarch to try to see to the conversion of all to the true faith, he ought to close his eyes and ears to the faults of the incorrigible and at least extract from them some useful work. i) In order to further the economy the importation of all luxury goods with the exception of spices should be prohibited; to encourage the development of commerce even further the nobility was to be convinced that there was nothing dishonorable about engaging in trade, and every merchant whose business brought in in excess of 100,000 florins yearly from abroad was to receive certain honors and privileges. j) Younger sons of the nobility were not in the position to serve the State if they were destitute. Hence they should not avoid even a mésalliance to restore their finances. There existed no biological differences between king, count, bourgeois, and peasant; bias and good qualities were the products of education and observation. k) Luxurious living was to be diminished drastically by, *inter alia,* a wholesale reduction of feast days, by sumptuary legislation which would require the military always to appear in public in uniform and other State employees in simple black suits, by limiting all official banquets to one course, and by a prohibition against serving foreign wines or foods. l) A number of reforms were to be undertaken to make the armed forces both more effective and more economical to maintain. m) On the military model all those who drew state pensions and were not actively engaged in State service were to be put on half pay; either military pay had to be raised or that of the civil servants lowered. n) It was high time that State ministers and councilors give up their disreputable, indifferent and lazy ways; they should work rather than waste their time at hunting, parties, gala dinners, and diverse spectacles. o) Chiefs of departments must be willing to train young men of good birth to succeed them one day, rather than to rely exclusively on subordinates of no social stature merely because these were willing to do all the work and were not in a position to comment audibly on the ignorance of their chiefs. p) A monarch could only gain a correct impression of the problems confronting him by seeing them at first hand, and he himself intended to travel incognito throughout his dominions.) He still recognized that to approve of everything that one's predecessors had done and to want to change everything were untenable extremes, but, on the whole, the second tendency commended itself rather more to him, although he was aware that it would take much courage and even more patriotism to be an innovator in his century. In closing, Joseph observed for Maria Theresia's benefit that all great changes should be accomplished dramatically and at once, as all change creates turbulence and the disturbance might as well be for something worthwhile. The ruler should inform the public of his intentions in full, but then should suffer no opposition, particularly from those who would be defending their private interests.

It is difficult to make sense of this bewildering document. It combines acute, penetrating observations of real evils and sensible recommendations for their alleviation with completely idiosyncratic touches, some bordering on *idées fixes,* along with the most superficial gleanings from several fields of knowledge of which the Emperor evidently did not have the remotest notion. It all reads like an essay written by a brilliant but unstable high school student on the subject "What would I do where I to become Emperor." But Joseph, at the time he wrote these reflections, was twenty-four years old, had many years' experience in the *Staatsrath* and contact with administrative agencies, and could not really give untrammeled freedom to his phantasy such as a schoolboy might, as he was in fact Emperor and thus had certain responsibilities. Was Joseph unaware of the almost ludicrously heterogeneous nature of his essay? Being an essentially humorless man, he probably made his jokes painfully broad whenever he was in a joking mood. It is not really credible that in this case he mastered sufficient subtlety to present his real gems in a sea of trivia in order to accentuate their worth.

Maria Theresia's reaction, as was only to be expected, was anything but favorable. She saw in Joseph's memorandum evidence that the deplorable ideas which he had already urged upon her some six years earlier, instead of having been discarded as youthful errors, had become ingrained in him. Only Kaunitz' observations that, while he disagreed with many of the Emperor's points, the memorandum nevertheless was a superlative indication of the young ruler's exceptional ability and of his nobility of heart, somewhat tempered her displeasure.[6] It has been maintained that it was this document, submitted by Joseph to his mother, that was responsible for her decision to take hold of herself, overcome her grief and return from the semi-obscurity which had enveloped her since her husband's death. This argument, while not unconvincing, overlooks the fact that the Empress even in her darkest moments had not intended to turn over all her powers to Joseph irrevocably. If he were now to address himself to the problems of the Monarchy in the sense which she intended, if he would refrain from attempting to change that which she considered to be fundamental to her system, she would be happy to show him how to play the leading role. She was by no means ready, however, to allow not only her person but her innermost convictions to be supplanted by innovations which she distrusted deeply. It was one thing to allow him a free hand in cutting down the expenses of the Court, abolishing the practice of maintaining separate tables for all the members of the Imperial family, reducing the number of horses kept by the Court almost by half, and ordering a general massacre of the boars in the environment of Vienna. It was quite another to allow Joseph to believe that he was free to wield his new broom among the innermost recesses of cherished Hapsburg tradition.

And even the relatively innocuous reforms that Joseph permitted himself in the early days of his co-regency met with virulent denunciation from those upon whose interests they infringed. When, for instance, he opened up the spacious and verdant Prater, the most beautiful of Vienna's parks and hitherto reserved for the use of the nobility, to the general public, the aristocrats complained long and loud about being forced to rub shoulders with *hoi polloi* even in their leisure moments. Joseph's rejoinder that, were he to insist on associating only with his equals, he would be forced to spend all his time in the Capucin crypt where his ancestors were buried, at least put them in their place for this once. But every one of Joseph's small reforms, each of his little economies was an infringement of some ancient vested interest. After there had been enough of these in a relatively short span, it became plausible to argue that what Joseph intended was an uncompromising revolution in which no part of the system would be spared. Maria Theresia was intelligent enough to realize that so far no really substantive changes had been attempted, but being in possession of Joseph's memorandum, she could convince herself in good conscience that he intended to abolish arbitrarily more than merely antiquated and unimportant privileges. And very likely he did.

How far the Emperor intended to go in 1765, whether he was really prepared to ignore the growing chorus of protest from the privileged orders, must remain in the realm of conjecture, as he was presently checked in his tracks. It is an exaggeration to maintain that "the old order had returned," [7] but there is no doubt that the Empress attempted to limit Joseph's power. But, of course, there could be no question of undoing all that had been done, or of reducing Joseph belatedly to the position of a nonentity. Consequently, Maria Theresia's return to more active control meant the beginning of a struggle between herself and her son which would last for the rest of her life. Unwilling to break with him completely, she would give in to him whenever he sufficiently identified himself with a position to press on to the point of threatening to leave. Thus that strangely ambivalent and for both sides frustrating relationship which characterized the co-regency began.

The key figure in this struggle was to be Prince Kaunitz. To him Maria Theresia had turned with Joseph's alarming memorandum, and his expositions had delineated the position which, without being quite able to formulate it, she wanted to occupy. It must not be overlooked that Kaunitz had a vested interest of his own to defend in the matter. After all, he had been in an exalted position in the government for some fifteen years, in a really dominant one for at least ten, and for him to concede to all of Joseph's strictures would be to condemn his own work. As a rival in the form of a Haugwitz was no longer on the scene, Kaunitz could not shed the responsibility for any inadequacies in the system by blaming his colleagues. If the system was hopelessly bad, the fault would be his. He took the line that while many of Joseph's arguments were meritorious, the spirit in which they were couched was immoderate. Changes were needed, but they should come within the framework of already existing institutions. The foundation for the no doubt necessary reforms already existed. His most telling argument, aimed unerringly at Maria Theresia's most tender sensibilities, was to the effect that Joseph proposed to establish a military despotism in the Prussian style.[8] This would have put her off even if she had not already felt a deep antipathy for the spirit which had guided Joseph. But Kaunitz had been careful to approve of enough of Joseph's proposals so that the Emperor would not regard him as merely another obstacle in his path. He had played the game in a truly masterly way. Henceforth both Maria Theresia and Joseph would be convinced that the Chancellor was in reality of a mind with them and that he occasionally endorsed the position of the other only out of respect for their person. Thus, so long as the Empress lived, Kaunitz could choose to lend his support only to these schemes of Joseph's which appeared useful to him in the light of the political position of the moment and still leave the Emperor with the impression that he was really on his side.

At this point it behooves us to ask what might have happened if Kaunitz had not succeeded in recalling Maria Theresia from the momentary apathy into which she had fallen at the death of her husband. In answer to this it is reasonable to suppose, in view of what actually happened some fifteen years later when the Empress died, that the Chancellor would not have attempted on his own to put a serious brake on the Emperor's ambition but would rather have resigned, or, more likely, adapted his own position to the new circumstances. What would have followed upon this is very difficult to say. If we judge Joseph's political and intellectual development from the memorandum of 1765, it had not yet reached a very advanced state. He was greatly annoyed with the clumsy and antiquated apparatus which he had inherited and was determined to modernize it. But he was not as yet aware even of the nature of the really fundamental evils that existed in the Hapsburg state. It is a mistake to speak of the memorandum as an attack upon feudal privilege.[9] A close reading will reveal that while it attacks the nobility for its all too frequent laziness and inefficiency, it does not begin to address itself to the question of whether perhaps the whole nature of land-holding within the State might not have to be drastically changed. These were considerations which presented themselves to Joseph only much later. Thus there appears to have been two diametrically opposed possibilities, had Joseph prevailed in 1765. He might have exhausted his energies by ramming through what was essentially a collection of trivialities, and seeing that this led nowhere he might have turned to other interests, perhaps foreign affairs. Or, he might have learned by doing, as in a way he did after 1780, and he would have understood that in order to achieve changes at the surface he would first have to change that which lay underneath; he would thus have arrived at essentially the same program which was to be, in part at least, the product of his long broodings during the co-regency. In that case, of course, assuming that his health would have held out as long as it in fact did, he would have had an additional fifteen years to devote to this work.

The sense of deadly urgency, of reckless haste, which was to mar much of his later work might not have been as strong, and his reforms, with him to oversee them and stand behind them for a quarter of a century, might well have turned out more robust than in fact they did. But all this must remain speculation. By the end of the year Maria Theresia had made it plain to him that thereafter he was to limit himself to the affairs of the army and of the Court. All other questions would remain in her province.

CHAPTER IV

The Co-Regency

THE EARLY YEARS OF THE CO-REGENCY WERE ANYTHING BUT HAPPY ones for Joseph. Apart from the continual frustrations he had to suffer at the hands of his mother, his personal life continued to be marred by tragedy. In 1767 his second wife Josefa died, also of the smallpox. Never a hypocrite, Joseph did not shed any tears for the woman he could not abide, but the conviction that in some unexplained way fate would not permit him to be happy with a woman seems to have taken hold of him. Certainly, he would never again suffer any talk of yet another marriage. A much harder blow was in store for him. At the beginning of 1770 his little daughter Maria Theresia became ill with what was soon diagnosed to be pneumonia. Joseph spent his days and nights at her bedside. In spite of Van Swieten's best efforts she did not improve. The little girl seemed to put up no more of a struggle against death than had her mother. After a week she was dead. Joseph, by now experienced as a mourner, did not publicize his grief as he had when Isabella died. But, as a sentient human being, he was finished. His touching cry, "Now I have ceased to be a father," could equally well have been "I am no longer a person." He showed every consideration for those who had served his daughter, pensioning them off handsomely in spite of his well-known aversion for unearned income. When, having ordered the Court to go into mourning, he was told by the Imperial Chamberlain Prince Khevenhüller that this was not the custom at the death of minor children, he at once countermanded his order.[1] On the other hand, he raged against Van Swieten, saying he never wanted to set eyes upon him again. But his lasting reaction was a mixture of cold despair and almost inhuman detachment. He was not meant to enjoy happiness like others, very well, he would not even try. Hereafter his work, his duty would have to suffice.

The exercise of what he considered to be his duty did not make things any easier for Joseph. When he reprimanded those whom he considered remiss in the performance of their functions, his reward was apt to be a long and hectoring lecture from his

[42]

mother. She accused him of modeling himself on Frederick of Prussia who for all his pains was forced to live in fear of everyone.[2] She saw Joseph's all too often deserved criticisms of her old servants as nothing more than the product of his willfully negative spirit. He was not yet, she told him in 1766, thoroughly misanthropic, but he was well on the way to reaching that end. Furthermore, she accused him of being an intellectual frump, who could not resist making every new and arresting thought his own and making immediate use of it whether it fitted a given situation or not. Although nothing could have been more unjust, as the Emperor undoubtedly held back the greater part of the critical remarks which the disorder he saw everywhere around him all but cried for, he answered softly and apologized humbly to his mother.[3] His tone was so submissive, so self-accusatory, that if his devotion to Maria Theresia were not established beyond a doubt one would suspect him of sly irony.

There was much to evoke the Emperor's criticisms in these years. True to his own precept that a ruler must see things for himself, he traveled to Hungary and to Bohemia. The misery of the peasants in both these lands surpassed by far anything which even the most sanguine advocates of agricultural reforms in Vienna could imagine. Maria Theresia herself was convinced that to strengthen the Monarchy it was necessary to raise up the peasants. She even talked in terms of freeing them from their shackles, making them independent proprietors. Proposals of this kind were regarded by the *Staatsrath*, as incompatible with the stability of the realm; even Joseph seemed to have his doubts about their practicality, and the Empress did not insist.[4] But in order to make at least a beginning, a law was promulgated in 1766 which regulated the amount of *robot*, or forced labor, which a landlord could require from his serf to three days weekly. Unfortunately, as the Emperor had only too ample opportunity to observe on his travels, this law was honored almost entirely in the breach.

In Hungary the nobles might convince themselves that their rustics could not be more content—"Your life is pure and sweet in innocence, your pleasures unmixed with any evil thoughts" [5] —but Joseph knew better. Complaints reached him that the peasants were forced into rendering five or even six days of socage (forced labor) weekly, and as the Church prevented them from working Sundays, how could they work their own acres? They could not even pay their taxes.[6] When Joseph pressed for more effective legislation, he was met with unconcealed hostility on the part of those whose interests would be adversely affected by this, and by an immobilism impervious to all argument in the *Staatsrath*. There, the position defended by Kaunitz among others was that the conditions of servitude and the obligations of the serfs throughout the various provinces of the Monarchy were so varied that no legislation could even hope to address itself to the whole. In consequence, before anything could be accomplished, further studies would have to be undertaken. This was not to be Joseph's first encounter with this time-honored device which every bureaucracy uses to explain away its inaction.

But the Emperor was not to be deterred. Once he had convinced himself that agricultural reform was necessary, he kept coming back to the subject. It should not be imagined that he acted only out of humane concern for his rustic subjects. While he was not without compassion, he, who did not shy away from brutally hard work himself, was not averse to his subjects also working to the limit of their capacities. But the peasants were being trodden into the ground and had ceased to be productive subjects. This was a consideration which would not be lost on a reader of the physiocrats, no matter how loudly he proclaimed his independence of all economic doctrine. Joseph won a number of small victories. In 1768 the landowners were forbidden to confiscate the food supply their serfs might have; in 1769 the 10 per cent tax which they had been placing on the fodder the serfs gleaned from fallow land was abolished, and the lords were made to provide food for any serfs they imprisoned. Finally, in 1771 an Urbarial Commission was created to arbitrate disputes arising between lord and serf.[7] Now at last there was an agency in being which could, if circumstances were propitious, arrogate a regulatory power, based on the necessity for creating conditions within which such disputes might reasonably be solved. The establishment of this Commission was Joseph's first great accomplishment in internal politics.

Joseph's other attempts to influence the course of affairs were less successful. In 1766, having examined the state of the Austrian armed forces, which Maria Theresia had turned over to him more or less as his private domain, he demanded a significant increase in numbers as the first step toward reform. He was put off by Kaunitz, who did not at that moment wish to complicate the political situation with arrant military preparations, with some platitudes about the necessity of keeping in balance one's armed forces, one's political plans, and one's resources. Joseph's efforts to insert himself into the lawyers' debates on the reform of the criminal code, debates which had been going on for years, were for the most part unavailing. When a new code was at last published in 1768, this so-called *Nemesis Theresiana* reflected only very dimly the Emperor's views. Nor, in truth, did it reflect those of the lawyers. They had, after some fifteen years of labor, presented for the Empress' approval a compilation in no less than eight folio volumes, which however did not get beyond the civil code. To the criminal code they proposed to address themselves at greater leisure. Kaunitz was justifiably appalled at this example of prolixity remarkable even in the legal profession and advised Maria Theresia to withhold her *placet*. Thereupon he created a second and much smaller body with instructions to come up with workable proposals for the reform of the criminal code within a year. Given the need for great hurry, it is perhaps not surprising that the *Nemesis Theresiana* did not differ greatly from previous codes. It provided the full catalogue of medieval horrors for a wide variety of crimes, and gave detailed instructions on how to carry out such punishments as quartering, burning alive, drowning, and impaling. The severest penalties were reserved for crimes of a religious nature: blasphemy, the robbing of churches, witchcraft, the practice of black magic, heresy, and apostasy; *lèse majesté*, treason, and the counterfeiting of State documents were also punishable by death. There were only two rays of light. One was that a number of mitigating circumstances were recognized, including not only noble birth or the knowledge of a useful trade, but also feeblemindedness, illness, youth, or outside compulsion. The other was the abolition of judicial torture, that is, torture before a verdict had been rendered in a case and meant to extract a confession.[8] This last advance redounded principally to the credit of the publicist Joseph Sonnenfels who had been agitating for this for years, but was also to a degree due to the efforts of Joseph.

Whatever the real nature of Joseph's position as co-regent, by 1769 he had convinced himself that his position was untenable, if not actually ludicrous. He objected, in particular, to placing his signature on public documents of which he did not approve, and begged his mother to excuse him from this highly unpleasant duty. As Joseph's ceasing to sign documents would have created a considerable stir, Maria Theresia begged him, for her sake, to desist from his demand. At first Joseph proved obdurate, but finally surrendered to Kaunitz, who argued with more truth than tact that since everyone knew that Joseph did not have the power to hold up legislation, his signature was a mere formality, not worth arguing about.

Perhaps the co-regent judged his own accomplishments too pessimistically. His mother was not implacable. If he really insisted on something, the likelihood was that she would give way, or at least be troubled sufficiently by her conscience to let him have his way in the very next argument. Maria Theresia was perhaps not once convinced that Joseph's proposals, which for the most part struck her as tempestuous, ill-considered, and likely to lead to immediate disaster, had any merit. But, as she grew older, the realization that he would soon be in the position to do as he wished anyway, led her to a sort of resignation. More and more she gave way to him, against her better judgment, often with loud protestations, but she gave way. For this reason, as we shall see, many of the great Josephinian reforms actually were begun, and in some cases completed, in the period of the co-regency. And there is every reason to believe that Joseph knew that he could, if necessary, prevail over his mother. His use of the ultimate threat of resignation suggests less a man at the end of his resources than a tactical motive. There were also those who thought that they could descry the handwriting on the wall. In all the larger towns of the Empire groups of liberally inclined thinkers began to form. They proceeded cautiously at first, as Maria Theresia made use of a large army of police spies, and to be reported for propounding a doctrine of the hated French Enlightenment could get one into serious trouble, but by the 1770s they had become bolder. They identified themselves with Joseph, and more or less in his name began to agitate openly against obscurantism and its dark emanations.[9]

This was actually safer than it might otherwise have been, as obscurantism could conveniently be equated with the Jesuits. The Society of Jesus, which since the hectic days of the Counter Reformation had enjoyed a practical monopoly over all intellectual and educational pursuits in the Austrian Monarchy, was currently held in a pungently bad odor. Like all great experiments, it had receded in intensity and purposefulness after its initial period of great creativity. Particularly in Austria, the Jesuits had succeeded perhaps too well, and secure in their power, they in many cases hardly bothered to go beyond a mechanical and routine performance of their functions. Furthermore, the Society now entertained political ambitions and aspired to such heights that its members did not hesitate to quarrel openly with the highest authority, the great monarchs of Europe. It was even whispered that the Pope himself was not immune from Jesuit pressure. The result was that at the beginning of the 1770s the principal Catholic courts of Europe, with the exception of Austria, had not only expelled the Society from their own lands but were putting pressure on the Papacy to dissolve it entirely. Maria Theresia, who had been educated by the Jesuits and who held them in the highest respect for their devotion to piety, refused to be drawn into this game, but it was quite impossible even for her to shield the Society from the increasingly violent attacks which, inspired by foreign example, were being made on it. Thus it was possible for one of her subjects, a man, let us say, of liberal inclinations, to defame the Jesuits almost at will, and to include in his indictment a number of complaints which, it would be clear to all his listeners, had nothing whatever to do with them.

As Joseph's liberal supporters were to find out with distressing regularity later on, the Emperor himself was no liberal. Moreover, his own attitude toward the Society had by no means been made clear. On the occasion of a visit to Rome in 1769, at a time when, the Pope having died, the cardinals were in conclave, he had not identified himself with either the pro- or the anti-Jesuit party. But he too had come to see the Society as a threat to the one cause which above all others he considered holy, the inviolability of the royal power. When the conclave elected Cardinal Campanelli, a Franciscan enemy of the Jesuits, as Clement XIV, it appeared that the moment to move against the Society was at hand. But the new Pope, by nature a peaceful man, was also wary of antagonizing Maria Theresia, and he temporized. Joseph in a letter to Louis XV's minister, the Duc de Choiseul, now revealed where he stood.[10] The Jesuits, whom he claimed to know as well as any man, he reviled not so much as obscurantists, but as a power-hungry folk who had arrogated unto themselves all real authority in Germany, in France, in Spain, in Paraguay. He himself was powerless to do anything against Maria Theresia's stubborn defense of the Society, but Kaunitz was anti-Jesuit and would doubtless be able to persuade the Empress in fairly short order.

The Chancellor was, as a matter of fact, an outspoken anticlerical, who managed to be this in spite of Maria Theresia's piety in part because he was always careful to represent his attacks upon the Church as defenses of the Imperial power. Already in

1770, in the course of an argument with the Papacy involving the age at which postulants should be admitted to monasteries, a subject which, incidentally, was very close to Joseph's heart, Kaunitz had submitted for the Empress' considerations a draft of a letter to Clement XIV in which he defended the Austrian Crown's right to legislate on this matter as stemming from its supreme power.[11] Maria Theresia had, to be sure, softened the blow on the grounds that she did not wish to issue a manifesto, but in the end Kaunitz achieved at least a partial victory.

Acting under Bourbon pressure, Clement XIV let it be known in October 1772 that he was willing to dissolve the Society of Jesus if he could secure the approbation of all the Catholic monarchs of Europe. Otherwise, he would run the risk of having the dissolution rejected by this or that Court. It was obvious that Austria was meant by this. Maria Theresia was the Jesuits' last hope. Charles III of Spain offered his services as honest broker to the Papacy, and composed a letter to the Empress in which he maintained that it would be highly displeasing to the Pope not to dissolve the Society.[12] Immediately thereafter Kaunitz presented Maria Theresia with a detailed proposal for an answer. The substance of it was that the Empress, in spite of her well-known admiration for the Jesuits, would not oppose the Pope's wish to dissolve the Society but that she would insist upon the right of disposing of their property as she thought best. And Joseph at once submitted a detailed proposal for making use of the resources of the Jesuits and for the performance of the duties which had formerly been their responsibility.[13] Once the bull *Dominus ac Redemptor* which dissolved the Society of Jesus was published, Maria Theresia professed to be in despair at the course she had been forced to follow.[14] Joseph undoubtedly was pleased, although his intemperate letter to the Spanish ambassador to France, Count Aranda, which is quoted in many serious accounts, is undoubtedly a forgery.[15] But the entire fortune of the Society, estimated at an excess of 400 million florins, in those days an utterly fantastic sum, was now to go into a special educational fund to be administered by the *Hofkammer,* and this prospect might well have elicited some genuine protestations of enthusiasm from the Emperor. But here he was to be bitterly disappointed. Taking advantage of Maria Theresia's undisguised sympathy for them and of the proverbial Austrian dilatoriness, the Society was able to convert a good part of its holdings into freely negotiable paper and when the various commissions destined to take over its property at last took up their work they more often than not found that the funds they were meant to take over were no longer there.[16]

While it is no longer possible to determine with certainty just to what degree Joseph had been influential in deciding Austrian policy toward the Jesuits, or to differentiate his views from those of Kaunitz, we are in a much better position to describe the Emperor's growing concern with the agricultural question in general, and the status of the peasantry in particular. We have seen that the problem preoccupied him already in the first years of his co-regency. What elevated it to a burning concern was the great Central European crop failure and famine of 1770–71, which, particularly in Bohemia and Moravia, quickly brought about conditions that can only be described as catastrophic.

The state of the Czech peasants had been a particularly hard one ever since Hapsburg rule in those provinces had become a tangible reality with the crushing defeat of the Czech Estates at the White Mountain in 1620. Loyal servants of the Monarchy had been rewarded with extensive Bohemian and Moravian estates. As these were often Austrians, Germans, Italians, Frenchmen, even Scots, who did not know the language of the country and were not disposed to learn it, they mostly left the administration of their holdings in the hands of native overseers. As this gentry had every intention of making its fortune too, the peasants often had to bear a double load. The central government, which in other parts of the Monarchy at least gave the serfs a minimal protection against the most rapacious demands of the landlords, seemed to be completely blind to conditions in these provinces. In 1738 Bohemian landowners had been granted concessions so sweeping that they amounted to unrestrained power over their peasants. Thereafter, if anything, things got worse. The loss of Silesia in the 1740s had necessitated a blanket 10 per cent increase in taxes throughout the Monarchy. But instead of an equitable distribution taking place, Bohemia and Moravia were made to shoulder 35 per cent of the total additional burden. The result was that these provinces were now made to bring in between 32 and 40 per cent of the total revenue of the Monarchy, four times as much as Hungary, a considerably richer province.[17] Understandably, the landowners who were made to pay these heavy imposts did all in their power to squeeze the last ounce of revenue out of their serfs. A commission under Count Von Trautmanns-dorff, sent to look into this situation in 1769, reported that the Czech peasants were destitute, brutalized, beaten frequently, and shamelessly exploited.[18] As eighteenth-century noblemen were not easily shocked by rural poverty, which they considered very much a part of the natural order of things, conditions in Bohemia must have been incredibly bad to elicit such a report.

On top of this came a partial crop failure in 1769, a terrible winter in 1770, and torrential rains in the spring of 1771 which destroyed the young crops in the fields. The price of grain actually reached a level five times as high as normal. There were no longer even roots to eat for the serfs. They ran away in increasing numbers, formed themselves into roving bands, and without much success attempted to plunder the destitute countryside. Decomposing bodies, which no one took the trouble to bury, littered the rural roads.[19] The provincial administration, whose duty it would have been to relieve this misery, was paralyzed, partly by the magnitude of the disaster, partly by the unfortunate circumstance that both the Chancellor of Bohemia, Chotek, and the Governor of Prague, Kolowrat, were superannuated, sick, and senile. The Court itself was finally forced to step into the breach. Maria Theresia ordered an embargo on the export of foodstuffs from the Czech provinces and set aside a sum of 3 million florins for the purchase of Hungarian grain to relieve the famine.[20] But these were half-measures and were moreover put into effect with the infuriating slowness so characteristic of the Austrian bureaucracy. Joseph, who had become increasingly disturbed by the frightening nature of the reports from Bohemia, vainly tried to force a quicker pace upon the unwilling officials. He complained to his brother Leopold about the "lethargy and apoplectic languor." [21] The Emperor decided that he would have to go to Bohemia himself in order to take charge personally of the relief work. But Maria Theresia refused to give him permission to go.

Joseph labored mightily under this restriction. The Empress' reasons for keeping him in Vienna were doubtless in the first instance maternal concern for his safety: it would surely be dangerous for him to travel in the midst of disease and civil disorder; and secondly, an understandable reluctance to allow him to put into operation the radical and direct measures which she knew him to favor. There is no reason to suppose that Joseph insinuated, with or without reason, that Maria Theresia was unwilling to allow him to gain general acclaim for himself by a successful intervention. Others too warned him of the hardships of his projected journey, but as he observed to one of these Cassandras, "kingship is a profession." Finally Maria Theresia gave in to his demands. By October 1771 he was in Bohemia, traveling on horseback with only a minuscule suite.

Joseph's first reaction to the incredible misery he saw on every side was characteristic. He complained that as the result of the famine the state of the country was such that the King of Prussia would have no difficulty in conquering it with no more than 20,-000 men. This circumstance, in turn, would now have a severely inhibiting effect on the whole of Hapsburg foreign policy.[22] Having reached Prague, he took stock of the situation. For the moment it was so desperate that immediate relief would have to be supplied and he proposed some measures meant to prevent a complete collapse which, he thought, seemed imminent. But, as he informed Maria Theresia, these were at best palliatives.[23] Back in Vienna, Joseph was appalled that his urgent recommendations were being acted on only very slowly, if at all. It was necessary for him to write volumes and preach and argue for hours before anyone could be persuaded to take so much as a single step.[24] The Emperor's complaints were answered by a remarkable letter from his mother. She confessed that she was old, tired, and discouraged, as well as devoid of ideas on how to meet the present crisis. She solicited his advice, praised his courage, and promised to support with all her influence those proposals which, after due reflection, he believed to be necessary. So long as Joseph would remain faithful to the divine law, she told him, she would continue to hope that he would emerge one day as the savior of his peoples.[25] It was thus at the express invitation of the Empress that Joseph now advanced his further recommendations. But, it must be said, it would have been highly uncharacteristic of him had he not exceeded the limits of even this very wide mandate.

Joseph first proposed a wholesale change of personnel in the principal departments concerned with economic administration, namely *Staatsrath, Hofkanzlei, Hofkammer, Bancodeputation,* and *Rechenkammer*. But, as he soon complained to Leopold, even with the best will in the world, the Empress was unable to overcome her inclination to good-heartedness, and the intrigues of those who would lose their positions had frustrated the whole project.[26] Anyway, the Emperor did not confine himself to *personalia*. His observations in Bohemia had convinced him that fundamental changes were necessary. To begin with, more funds than over the long run could be diverted from Vienna would be necessary to bring about a general recovery of the economy. In consequence, he proposed that a fund for this purpose be created out of the very considerable holdings of the Church in the Czech lands. This, of course, would have been crass expropriation, and as such was not apt to be acceptable to Maria Theresia. Beyond

this the Emperor saw that the really basic evil was the total subjection of the peasants. So long as the *robot,* the forced labor the
rustics owed their lords, was of such a magnitude that it prevented them from working their own lands, the situation was beyond repair. Consequently, Joseph agitated ceaselessly for the introduction of legislation which would regulate the amount of
robot that could be demanded of the peasantry. The Czech landowners, however, made their influence in the councils of state felt
and for a long time blocked any effective discussions, not to speak
of actual measures which could have prejudiced their position.
Curiously, Maria Theresia was willing to go further than Joseph
in this vital area. As she told Kaunitz, were it not for the obstacles
which appeared insuperable, she would much rather do away
with serfdom entirely than merely regulate the *robot.* The prospect of perhaps one day achieving this great goal was the only
consideration which kept her from giving up her position as head
of the State.[27]

But Joseph was not to be moved in the direction of a complete
abolition of serfdom. It is not clear whether this was because he
believed sincerely that not the system but its shameful exploita-
tion by the landowners was at fault, or because he was at this
point still of the opinion that the nobility was the only class with
and through which the State could accomplish its objectives.
What unquestionably did ensue was that, with Empress and co-
regent of two basically different opinions, the opponents of any
change at all had their task greatly simplified. Nothing perceptible happened for some two years. Joseph on occasion gave way to
expressions of complete despair. He complained that he was at his
desk from early morning until five or six in the evening but accomplished nothing. He told Leopold that he would gladly trade
with him, he would not even insist on his dish of lentils for the
rights of the elder.[28]

The situation, however, was not quite as hopeless as Joseph in
his darker moods imagined. The concatenation of a number of
factors eventually began to produce some results. In the first
place, Maria Theresia, seeing that her dream of emancipating the
serfs was not to be, swung around to support Joseph's demands
for reform of the existing system. Already in June 1773 she ordered that some sort of measures, either provisional or permanent, be undertaken for the relief of the Bohemian serfs. This led
the Bohemian Estates, in October, to overreach themselves. They
declared that they would accept no regulation whatever that infringed upon their ancient rights. When there was a sharp reac-

tion in Vienna to this piece of impertinence, the Estates temporized with proposals which manifestly would not have altered the
state of affairs. This intransigent attitude served only to unite
influential members of the Court aristocracy behind Joseph's
plans. Also, it should not be forgotten that in politics too, inertia
has both a positive and a negative aspect. It might have been
extremely difficult to move the various ministries, commissions,
and standing committees which claimed to be concerned in any
steps involving a basic change in the social order, but once they
had, with Herculean labors, been put into motion, it would have
been equally difficult to prevent them from accomplishing at least
some change.

The result of all this was the Urbarial Patent of April 1774. It
ordered all landowners to reach, within six months, new agree-
ments with their serfs about the amount of labor these were to
perform. In theory maximal demands, which were not to be exceeded, were set down, but these were set so high that they could
be of little practical value.[29] And even this went too far for the
landowners. In June they used their influence in Vienna to extort
a concession that in certain cases the maximum could be surpassed. This indecision and these half-measures were all but designed to create trouble, and the trouble was not long in coming.
The peasants of Bohemia had for some time been fed on vague
and exaggerated rumors of the benefits which would accrue to
them from Vienna. When these benefits proved to be largely imaginary, when in some cases the exactions demanded of them
even increased, they answered, in ever greater numbers, by refusing to perform any services at all. When there was no immediate
and forceful reaction from the authorities to these gross breaches
of discipline, they felt encouraged to go further and banded together in mutinous and threatening groups which roamed the
countryside. By the end of 1774 Bohemia was on the verge of an
open rebellion.[30] There were reports that in some cases mutinous
peasants had renounced their Catholic religion and were openly
confessing the old Hussite heresy. The leaders who emerged, as
under these circumstances they were bound to, claimed that they
soon would receive help from the King of Prussia and threatened
to lead a mass emigration out of Bohemia unless their demands
were met. By the spring of 1775 large bands of rebels were burning castles and churches and beating up those noblemen and
priests who fell into their hands.

So far the Government in Vienna had proceeded with extreme
caution. Not only was the Empress herself convinced that the de-

mands of the peasants were to a considerable degree justified, but the threats of Prussian intervention and mass emigration from areas already depopulated by the recent famine could not be taken lightly. But when the peasants began to make use of open violence, they could no longer be ignored. The army commanders in Bohemia, who had already received considerable reinforcements, were ordered to crush the uprising. This they succeeded in doing with relatively little difficulty, as the peasants had never been able to put their hands on any significant quantities of arms.

The aftermath of this sad business was a complex one. Maria Theresia decided that the troubles had been the result of her own inability to take hold after the death of her husband, her increasing lassitude brought on by advancing old age, her old woman's weakness. It was time for her to go. Joseph was partly responsible for what had happened, as he had made irresponsible promises in the spheres of religion and social obligations of the peasants, but once he had the sole power he would also have the sole responsibility. When he could no longer hide behind her, he would recognize that it was impossible to speak openly of things which could not be accomplished.[31]

It is by no means clear whether Maria Theresia ever communicated this decision to Joseph. At any rate, she soon changed her mind. It was, after all, her duty to remain on the throne so long as the Almighty still required her services, no matter how unpleasant they might be. Soon afterward Joseph was complaining that no decision about the Czech questions could be wrung out of the Empress.[32] Ten times she had given various orders and then again countermanded them. It was now high time that something were done. The only way to put an end to the troubles there was to do away with the confusion which prevailed on all sides in the matter of the *robot* obligations. If the *robot* were, as he had previously urged, reduced to a maximum of three days a week, the peasants would be satisfied and the landlords could be compensated by a corresponding increase in the ground rent, which in turn the peasants would be able to afford from the greater profit they would earn on their own land. Before long the landlords would themselves realize that it was to their advantage to convert the *robot* entirely into money payments, as had long ago been done in more progressive lands.[33] Kaunitz now objected that it was unseemly for a ruler to grant his rebellious subjects concessions, thus making such concessions appear to be a reward for their mutinous behavior. A Baron Kressl was now dispatched to

Bohemia to have another look at the situation. He reported that the rebellion had been due entirely to the disappointed expectations of the peasantry. It would serve no real purpose now to introduce Draconian repressions. It would suffice to deport a few of the ringleaders.

At last Maria Theresia reached a decision which corresponded much more closely to Joseph's position than to her own. In August 1775 a new patent regulating the *robot* was proclaimed. It had a close resemblance to the proposals with which the Emperor had identified himself. Moreover, in the Imperial estates, in accordance with a proposal made some ten years earlier by Karl Anton von Raab, serfdom was abolished completely and the peasants were permitted to rent small parcels for their own use. They were also permitted to receive loans which would enable them to rent the necessary agricultural implements. No doubt it was hoped that this example would be followed by lesser landholders.[34]

Joseph had thus, in the main, prevailed. It was unfortunate, however, that these measures proved to be almost entirely unrealistic. Not only did the landowners fail to imitate the example of the Crown, but they put up a for the most part effective resistance to the provisions of the new patent. The Emperor would be forced to return to the subject before long.

CHAPTER V

Education, Religious Toleration, Travels

AMONG THE SUBJECTS TO WHICH JOSEPH DEVOTED HIMSELF MOST AS-
siduously during his co-regency was education. By the time he was
twenty he was firmly convinced that the influential elements in
Austrian society could only be persuaded to accept the changes
which he believed to be necessary if, through education, they
themselves were made aware of their necessity. Traditionally, education on all levels in Austria had been in the hands of the
Church, particularly of the Piarist Fathers and the Jesuits. Long
before the dissolution of the last named society, complaints about
the deficiencies of the system had begun to accumulate. The quality of instruction, the preparation of the teachers, the breadth of
subject matter taught were far behind those of other European
countries. This circumstance particularly could not fail to infu-
riate the Emperor.

Already before 1770 Count Johann Anton von Pergen, who
had been brought to Vienna as his special assistant by Prince
Kaunitz and later was appointed as Director of the Oriental
Academy, had drawn up a comprehensive report dealing with
secondary education.[1] The main points of the report were that
one should do all in one's power to attract into the educational
establishment true but also enlightened and capable Christians;
to extend the authority of the State over all aspects of education;
and to relieve the regular clergy (including the Jesuits) of all
their educational functions, replacing it with either secular clergy
or lay teachers. Joseph greeted these suggestions with alacrity and
was of the opinion that one should start with them forthwith in
the academies devoted to the educating of the sons of the nobility. But the more conservative element at Court, particularly
Count Blümegen, objected that it would be much more sensible
and considerably cheaper to entrust the experienced regular
clergy with whatever reforms were necessary. Maria Theresia's
decision, rendered in April 1771, was characteristic: Pergen was
to submit a second and less ambitious plan, along with recommendations about how it might best be put into effect; in the

meantime he could try his proposals out at the Oriental Academy.

At this point, however, it turned out that Pergen was anything but subservient or timorous. He protested sharply against what appeared to him a total emasculation of his proposals, and so far convinced the Empress that she created a General Educational Commission (*Schuloberdirektorium*) and placed Pergen at its head. But she insisted that the regular clergy not be removed from its positions before a complete plan for educational reform had been worked out in detail and had been accepted.[2] As Pergen regarded this last as the operant clause, he declared that he could not assume this new position under these conditions. At this point Baron von Kressl, who was regarded by Maria Theresia as particularly reliable in educational questions, entered into the dispute. He argued that there was no question that reform was needed. He himself, at the age of twenty-one, had been unable to read the simplest Latin author, although he for six years had attended a *Gymnasium* which had been devoted to practically nothing but the study of Latin. But it would be preferable to proceed more gradually by introducing the needed reforms into the existing schools. Or, perhaps, with this threat in the air the regular clergy would on its own initiative reform its schools, and this would be an even better solution. Thereupon the Empress confirmed her previous decision. Her only concession was to order that Sonnenfels should begin a course of lectures in pedagogics at the University of Vienna, which would enable those teachers who felt the need to improve their abilities.

Pergen still refused to give in and protested against this decision as well. At this point Joseph again entered into the argument. In a memorandum dated July 1772 he took a stand which, although it was an accurate reflection of his purely empirical views on education, could hardly have pleased the advocates of enlightenment for enlightenment's sake.[3] Pergen's proposals, he said, appeared far too ambitious to him. The importation of renowned scholars might one day be useful, but what was important at the moment was to teach all subjects to read, to write, and a little bit of arithmetic. This would be useful particularly for the lower classes who could then serve the State with better effect, be it in business, in commerce, or in the army. Pergen's proposals were definitely rejected and he himself was kicked upstairs as governor of the recently acquired province of Galicia.

The dissolution of the Jesuits, however, which followed shortly upon these events, brought the whole question of the staffing of schools once again to the fore. Professor Anton von Martini of the University was now charged with the submission of further proposals. He started with the premise that every subject of the Monarchy should receive an education in keeping with his position in society and his chosen profession. At the same time the educational establishment should strive to inculcate in every student a spirit of national loyalty (*Nationalgeist*). To ensure that these objectives were achieved, the State should create a fund sufficient to pay for the educational establishment and supervise it at all levels. This came back in essence to Pergen's proposals, argued from the opposite direction. Perhaps for that reason, this plan too was rejected. Finally, the Piarist monk Gratian Marx was charged with submitting yet another proposal. It should surprise no one that what he proposed was merely to subject the existing system to an overhaul. This was then done. Secondary education was improved, but not markedly.

Somewhat happier was the situation with regard to elementary education. Here the old notion that even a modicum of education might encourage the lower classes to refuse to perform the hard and sometimes debasing labor that society required of them, had for some time been giving way to the insight that a subject who could at least read and write was more valuable to the State than one who could not. Already in 1771 a model school was opened in Vienna, which taught an expanded curriculum consisting not only of the usual rudiments but also of geography, history, and ethics.[4] Shortly thereafter Johann Ignaz Felbiger, who was abbot of the monastery of Sagan in Prussian Silesia and had made something of a name for himself with his rational methods of instruction, was imported for the purpose of reforming the Austrian elementary schools. He quickly worked out a program which was then incorporated into the so-called *Allgemeine Schulordnung* of December 1774. This last piece of legislation created three different types of elementary schools, which were to be attended by children of different backgrounds and prospects. But every child up to the age of thirteen was to attend school for at least four months of the year. Thus Felbiger created, unobtrusively and almost as an afterthought, the first truly universal educational system in Europe. Contrary to what is sometimes asserted, Joseph did not have much to do with these important changes.[5] Perhaps he was of the opinion that so long as the reform of elementary education was in the hands of a regular cleric such as Felbiger not much good could be expected to come of it anyway. Be that as it may, he only took an active interest in these matters when it was proposed to extend Felbiger's system to schools catering to the children of military officers. At that point he took violent exception to the proposal, objecting that this would lead inevitably to a breakdown of military discipline and that it was evident that the proponents of this step had not the least notion of what the army was all about. One could only say about them, "Forgive them, Father, for they know not what they do."

It will thus be seen that in the educational reforms of the Theresian period Joseph was anything but the prime mover, and that when he did take an interest in them he was by no means always to be found on the side of the angels. His chief concern seems to have been that the people receive enough education to make them into more useful subjects of the State. The regular clergy was to be relieved of its pedagogic function because it was suspect of putting loyalty to the Church above that to the State, but beyond this unnecessary subtleties and complications were to be avoided. This becomes clear as well from the Emperor's views about the reform of higher education, a step which was even more urgently necessary than the reform of the lower schools.

The University of Vienna, which in 1965 observed its six-hundredth anniversary, is the second oldest in Central Europe. But, in spite of its antiquity and great traditions, in the eighteenth century it had sunk into a seemingly permanent sleep. The Jesuits, who during the Counter Reformation had achieved complete control with the exception only of the medical faculty, were content to enjoy their prominent positions and not to risk any potentially dangerous experiments. The interesting and provocative questions which were being hotly debated at Leyden, at Cambridge, at Paris, had in many cases not even been heard of in Vienna. The attack upon the Jesuit maladministration of the University had been begun in the 1750s, principally by Van Swieten. By 1759 he had succeeded in convincing Maria Theresia that outsiders should be appointed to the directorships of the various faculties. The next decade saw the appointment to chairs at the university of several men not unfamiliar with the doctrines of the French Enlightenment. Paul Josef Riegger taught that the responsibility of maintaining order in the religious sphere rested not with the Church but with the State and that the persons and property of ecclesiastics were subject to the authority of the latter. His pupil Karl Anton Martini went even further in extending the competence of the State over important areas and finished by supplying the philosophical system which was to underlie the *étatisme* of Joseph.[6] The reformer Joseph Sonnenfels not only lectured at the University, but his courses in public administration were required of all those entering government service. But here too the Emperor's role was an ambivalent one.[7] Although he undoubtedly furthered the activities of some of the more liberal spirits, particularly Martini and Sonnenfels, he did not have much esteem for higher education in general. He was, in fact, of the opinion that university professors were for the most part overpaid and that it would be a good thing to remove the University from Vienna to some city in the provinces so that the scholars would not be forever tempted to neglect their studies in favor of the business of the State, which was no concern of theirs.

A question inevitably related to education was religious tolerance. By the middle of the eighteenth century most Catholic countries had accepted the verdict of the Thirty Years' War and were no longer attempting to extirpate their Protestant subjects, not even to make life so difficult for them that they they would either recant or emigrate. Even France, which had fought on the side of the Protestant states and then had all but eradicated its sizable Huguenot minority, was beginning to relent. The descendants of those Protestants who had survived the dragonnades, the revocation of the Edict of Nantes, and the attendant persecutions now enjoyed at least a semi-official toleration. The Austrian situation was, in its way, as complicated and paradoxical as the French. Austria had been throughout the bulwark of the Catholic side in the Thirty Years' War. Yet, because of its intricate mosaic structure Austria incorporated not unimportant Protestant minorities, some of which had to be tolerated by virtue of privileges going back to the sixteenth century, others having been guaranteed their right to existence by the Peace of Westphalia. These Protestants were barred from government service and suffered other disadvantages, but no attempt was made to inferfere with their freedom of worship, not even in the reigns of Leopold I or Charles VI, both of whom were surrounded by generally obscurantist advisers. It was a further paradox that Maria Theresia, who certainly far surpassed her predecessors in human sympathy and understanding and also lived in a time of general and increasing latitudinarianism in religious questions, should have been responsible for a considerable hardening in the official attitude vis-à-vis the Protestants. The explanation for this circumstance is not difficult to find. In her piety, her devotion to the Church, she could not see religious deviation as anything but a willful rejection of the universal truth necessary for salvation.

Those who would not believe out of their own free will would have to be compelled to do so for the good of their immortal souls. And the Empress lacked the cynicism which at times led others to allow a percentage of their subjects to proceed to what they regarded as certain damnation simply because it suited the interest of the State to avoid religious difficulties.

Legally, the situation was complicated also. The ordinances of 1752 had abrogated the various privileges which the Protestants of the Czech lands of the Monarchy still enjoyed. But these ordinances had never been systematically enforced.[8] Moreover, with the discomfiture of the Jesuits an unmistakable anticlericalism had manifested itself in the high councils of state in spite of the Empress' predilections. These attitudes found their expression eventually in legislation. After 1767 no papal bulls were any longer valid in Austrian territory without the Imperial *placet*. In 1773 the *Staatsrath* addressed a petition to Maria Theresia in which it humbly urged her to accord milder treatment to the Protestants. There were, it seemed, so many crypto-Protestants in her dominions that it was inconceivable to think of punishing them all.[9] Finally, Prince Kaunitz, possibly as a result of certain resentments stemming from his quarrel with the Church over the administration of Lombardy, possibly because of his contacts with a liberal discussion group in Vienna meeting at the house of a certain Provost Ignatz Müller, was developing a policy which, consequently applied, would result in the eventual complete subjection of the Church to the State. The result of all this was that the Draconian prohibitions of Protestantism were being more or less openly flaunted.[10]

This state of affairs was called to public attention when, as we have seen, the disturbances of 1775 in Bohemia took on an unmistakably anti-Catholic aspect. This was too much for Maria Theresia. Her acquiescence in the semi-toleration of the Protestants had always been a grudging one. When in 1770, she heard that some Protestant rowdies in Wetzlar had interfered with a Catholic procession, she remarked, almost wistfully, that no measures were too petty for her opponents, if only they were useful. Now that Protestantism had appeared in combination with open rebellion against secular authority, she was determined to make an end of it. She informed Joseph that there were three cardinal sins which she was determined not to accept: the free exercise of religion; the destruction of the existing authorities; and the freedom for her subjects to do anything they liked.[11]

Joseph answered that he would gladly abandon his principles

which so distressed his mother, if only he could be persuaded that
they were mistaken. As, however, he did not foresee this possibility, he asked to be relieved of his responsibilities as co-regent. He
could not be disobedient, but neither could he change his innermost convictions.[12] The Empress answered in turn that she could
not take up so unpleasant a subject during the holy and glorious
Christmas season. She would let him know her decision later.[13]
Joseph persisted. He demanded to be relieved of his duties and
adopted a distinctly unpleasant attitude to all those with whom
he had dealings.[14] Maria Theresia then threatened to resign. Kaunitz took umbrage at one of Joseph's sallies and let it be known
that he proposed to resign. The upshot of all this was that no one
resigned. An uneasy truce was patched up and for the time being
no overt measures were taken against religious dissidents.[15]

The truce did not last long. In 1777 some ten thousand Moravian crypto-Protestants chose this moment to declare their allegiance openly to their true religion. Maria Theresia informed Joseph, who happened to be traveling abroad, of this and solicited
his advice about what steps should now be taken. His answer,
perhaps the most complete declaration of his position in matters
of religion, deserves to be drawn upon in some detail. These
events, he said, only convinced him more strongly of the correct-
ness of his principles. It was necessary to establish complete liberty of conscience or to remove from the State all those who did
not believe as the ruler did. Did it really make sense, in order to
save the souls of those who did not want to be saved to deprive
the State of excellent farmers and obedient subjects? How could
one arrogate unto oneself the power to command the consciences
of men? The State could not do so with laws. He did not believe
that he could ever depart from this manner of thinking.[16]

The Empress was deeply offended. She wrote to Joseph, saying
that this letter would reach him in Switzerland, a place of asylum
for dissolutes and criminals. There he could see for himself the
consequences of religious liberty. Joseph's detestable notions
would fail to produce the practical advantages he expected of
them and would only result in the damnation of countless souls.
What was needed was true faith, inflexible rules.[17] Joseph's answer to this was carefully designed to turn away his mother's
wrath. She had, he wrote, misunderstood his use of the term toleration. God preserve him from being indifferent to whether his
subjects became Protestants or remained Catholics. He would
give everything he owned if every last one of them were to become a Catholic. By toleration he meant only that in purely secu-

lar matters he proposed to allow anyone who could be of use to the State to cultivate his lands or to pursue his business. It was far worse for Protestants to remain in their heretical lands than to live in the midst of Catholics where they would see for themselves the advantages of the true faith. Once there, moreover, if they were hindered in the free exercise of their religion, they might give up religion entirely, which was a far greater danger. In the end the result of toleration would be that all his subjects would be converted to Catholicism.[18]

Maria Theresia was not convinced. Toleration, she answered, was the equivalent of indifference. Without a dominant religion there would be no brake on the behavior of her subjects apart from the gallows or the wheel. Lawlessness would follow inevitably. But even worse, by arguing as he did, Joseph was endangerous the salvation of his own soul. He was on the point of destroying himself, and of dragging the entire Monarchy to perdition along with him. She did not propose to act in the spirit of persecution, but, as her ancestors had done before her, she would foster the Catholic religion with infinite care, effort, and expense. She hoped that Joseph would finish by doing the same and would turn away from false arguments and bad books. The liberty he proposed to introduce was unreal. It could result only in the complete overthrow of everything.[19]

But the Empress' determination to avoid the spirit of persecution proved anything but unshakeable. She presently dispatched troops to Moravia to achieve the reconversion of the apostates, having become convinced that there were Prussian agents at work in Moravia in behalf of Protestantism. Joseph might have been able to prevent this, but he was far away in France. The presence of troops seems to have helped in preventing further departures from the Catholic Church, but those who had already left it refused obstinately to rejoin it. The Empress now decreed that the recusants were to be inducted into the army or put to work building fortifications or imprisoned. Those unmoved even by these punishments were to be deported to the farthest mountains of Hungary, but not to Transylvania where prospects of reconversion would be extremely dim.[20]

By this time Joseph had not only returned from his travels abroad but happened to be on a military inspection tour of Moravia. He was appalled when he learned of these decisions, and this time there was nothing involute or scholastic about his protest.[21] The attempt to convert people by sending them to the mines had not been made since the start of the Reformation and would have incalculable consequences. Only the most stupid and shortsighted of the Empress' ministers could have given her such advice. Unless she consented to repeal these decrees at once he would resign on the spot. He could not suffer that such things happened during his co-regency and he would insist on letting the world know that he had nothing whatever to do with them. Maria Theresia answered that she had acted upon the recommendation of the competent organs, the Bohemian branch of the Chancellery and the *Staatsrath*. She was deeply hurt by Joseph's habit of threatening to resign at every difference of opinion. She reminded him that they owed an accounting to no one but Him Who had put them in their place and Whose holy law it was their duty to uphold. Joseph's reply to this was that if the measures he considered so odious had the full approval of the Empress he could only obey. But he could, given these conditions, no longer remain in his position. His protests did at least have the effect of staying the execution of the punitive legislation. He let it be known that he would not give way and that if these measures were carried out over his protests he would inform everyone who would listen that this was being done against his wishes.

The Moravian Protestants now decided to appeal directly to the Emperor.[22] It was his habit to receive in the Hofburg in Vienna anyone who wished to present a petition or a complaint. The delegates from Moravia asked Joseph to use his influence with his mother to secure for them freedom of conscience and the uninterrupted exercise of their religion. When Maria Theresia learned of this she promptly caused the delegates to be arrested. But with this she had gone too far. If Joseph's right to receive petitioners were to be abrogated, his position as co-regent would in truth have become untenable. The Empress would have to give way. As often happened during the co-regency when mother and son had reached an impasse, Kaunitz had the last word. In this instance he sided with Joseph. He argued first that it was inconceivable that the Church should be arrogating unto itself privileges, *i.e.* the use of force in religious questions, which Christ and the Apostles had explicitly rejected. Therefore, in passing, it surpassed his comprehension that the restrictive ordinance of 1754 could ever have come into being. At any rate, true faith is a gift of God and can not be compelled by force. In the case of the Moravians what was of importance was only whether they were merely guilty of unfortunate religious errors but otherwise comported themselves quietly, peacefully, and in keeping with their positions, or whether they also engaged in overt acts detrimental to the public order. If only the former were the case, there was nothing to do but to leave them in peace and to trust that the work of a conscientious Catholic clergy would ultimately succeed in reconverting them.[23] Not wanting to push the quarrel with Joseph further, Maria Theresia gave way.

There is no reason to doubt Joseph's protestations of his own Catholic convictions. If he nevertheless took the part of the Protestants, and was to do so even much more convincingly later, it was because he firmly believed that the interest of the State must be considered first and also because he probably had no wish to appear as a ridiculous obscurantist in the eyes of an increasingly enlightened West.

In this last matter, the Emperor's attitude was far from straightforward or uncomplicated. His attitude toward the enlightened ideas and the "modern" institutions of Western Europe had something of a then not yet classical attraction-repulsion aspect to it. Perhaps this ambivalence was a function of Joseph's attitude toward France. Although he, like every gentleman of his day, had received an education at least outwardly influenced by the French spirit, and although he had an undeniable taste for the ideas of a number of French thinkers, he had also an undisguised antipathy for France. This was in part the result of his conviction that the alliance with France had failed to produce any tangible results for Austria, and in part based on his dislike for the artificiality and pretentiousness to which high French society had been increasingly subject as the century advanced. Certainly it would be off the mark to maintain that he looked to the French for inspiration and example in order to modernize his own more backward domains. His attitude toward France was above all one of suspicion.

With all this, the Emperor was still drawn to France. Inveterate traveler that he was, he had never been to the country which everyone called the hub of Europe. Already in 1774 he expressed an interest in visiting France, but desisted from his intention because he feared that this might produce complications with Frederick of Prussia. Two years later, however, there were a number of sound political reasons for such a trip. In the first place, the precarious European equilibrium, so much disturbed by the appearance of Russia as a great European power toward the middle of the century, was threatening to break down once again. The Russians had recovered quickly from the period of confusion resulting from the brief but disastrous intervention of mad Peter III, and his widow Catherine II gave every indication of wanting to assert herself in the most positive way. During the past few years and under her dynamic leadership Russia had exerted strong pressure on the steadily declining Turks. It now appeared that Turkey might collapse entirely and Joseph was anxious to convince the French that the danger was real. Moreover, all did not seem to be going well with the marriage of Joseph's sister Marie Antoinette to Louis XVI, who had mounted the French throne in 1774. Disquieting reports had reached Vienna about the Queen's unpopularity with her subjects, and what was worse, there was no sign of an heir. The Austrian ambassador at Versailles, Count Florimond Mercy, hinted discreetly that it would first be necessary for the King to undergo a small operation. Altogether, it seemed to Joseph that his presence might well have beneficial effects.

The Emperor does not seem to have discussed his plans with his mother. At any rate, she complained that rumors of his impending visit to France were heard all over Vienna, but he had told her nothing. But even though she was somewhat reluctant to see Joseph go, the prospect of his putting to right a painful situation within her family was for her a compelling one.[24] When, at the end of 1776, the Elector of Bavaria, Max Joseph, who did not have any direct heirs, fell gravely ill, the Emperor's visit was decided upon. It had long been thought in Vienna that his death would be the opportune moment to press some Austrian claims in the matter of the Bavarian succession, and for this the support of France would be required.

As was his custom, Joseph traveled simply.[25] Under the incognito of Count Falkenstein he arrived in Paris in a single coach, accompanied only by a valet. Instead of installing himself at Versailles he stopped at an unpretentious hotel near the Luxembourg Palace. When he called upon his sister at Versailles he made no effort to disguise his disapproval of her frivolous habits. His opinion of Louis was not entirely unfavorable. He described him as a rather well-meaning and by no means ignorant man, handicapped by an unfortunate exterior and a complete lack of education. He was led around by the nose by those who knew how to take advantage of his complete apathy and lack of curiosity. He reminded one a little of inchoate matter before the coming of the *fiat lux*. He was powerless to change the course of policy, he could change only his servants. An aristocratic despotism reigned, with every minister absolute master in his department, but always in fear of being replaced. The result was that every minister was most concerned not to attract undue attention, which generally resulted in dismissal, but to steer a safe and conservative course. In short, the King had the absolute power only to pass from slavery to one minister to that of another. As an analysis of the system of Louis XIV in the absence of a Louis XIV this would have earned for Joseph the laurel in any academy of political science, but it is of course absurd to suggest that the Emperor in any way encouraged those critics of the regime who would, a dozen years later, achieve its overthrow.[26] In all his contacts he was extremely careful to be reserved in the expression of his opinions. When, at a social gathering, a lady was bold enough to ask him what he thought of the cause of the American rebels, which was extremely popular in France, his reply was: "Alas, madam, it is my profession to be a king." His simplicity of manner, his lack of ostentation, his simple costume of unadorned brown velvet undoubtedly caused some envious speculation about how cheaply one could support such a king, but the French, as Mme. du Deffand observed, soon tired of simplicity. Moreover, Joseph was extremely niggardly in the distribution of gratuities, and this failing was a grave one in France.[27]

Joseph spent most of his time in Paris visiting public institutions. While he paid a call on Rousseau, who at the time was copying music, and made ceremonial visits to the more important academies, he by no means occupied himself exclusively, or even to any considerable degree, with the *philosophes*. He was more interested in seeing how the administrative problems common to any great nation were mastered in France. He went on a tour of the provinces, and busied himself looking at canals, fortresses, and above all the commercial activity of the great French ports, which he envied unashamedly.[28]

As for those considerations which had originally prompted his visit, the Emperor achieved unequal results. In the diplomatic sphere, he accomplished nothing. Louis' foreign minister, the Comte de Vergennes, was of the opinion that the Austrian alliance had been a mistake when it was concluded, and was not of a mind to be drawn into adventures which would profit France but little. He professed to be convinced that after the late war the Russians were as exhausted as the Turks and that therefore there existed at the moment no threat of a decisive shift in the balance of power. Any action in concert with Austria would be, at the least, premature. As for the Bavarian question, the French had the gravest misgivings, although these were not really communicated to Joseph. He was merely given an evasive answer. Only from the point of view of family matters could Joseph's visit have been called a success. It did not take him long to find out that, apart from requiring a slight surgical intervention, the King had been guilty of inexcusable laziness and lack of ambition in the conjugal bed. The Emperor sternly lectured the young couple and the result was that within the year Marie Antoinette could write her mother that she was at last expecting an heir.

Joseph came home from France not dissatisfied with what he had seen and learned. He had been shrewd enough to put his finger on some of the more evident weaknesses in the government of that nation, but it would be a gross exaggeration to maintain that he in any way foresaw the catastrophe which was so near. France was then, as now, prosperous and it would have taken a much shrewder observer to discern that very prosperity as perhaps the most disequilibrating element in its political make-up.

On his way home Joseph, as we have seen, passed through Switzerland. As his route took him within a few miles of the home of Voltaire, it was expected by everyone that he would stop to visit the sage of Fernay. Voltaire made elaborate preparations to receive him. Instead, the Emperor ordered his coachman to drive on. The slight might well have been caused by Joseph's annoyance with Voltaire's attacks upon religion, or may have been a concession to the sensibilities of Maria Theresia. Or perhaps, the Emperor was merely availing himself of an opportunity to *épater les philosophes*.

The various frustrations of the co-regency were unrelieved by any personal joy for the Emperor. After the death of his first wife and of his daughter he withdrew into himself. The unfortunate experience of his second marriage turned him into a misogynist as well. He complained to Leopold about the incredible silliness of women. It was necessary for someone who really wanted to know his subjects to be constantly aware of this. Women were lazy and superficial and only the ardor of the moment made it possible for a lover to overlook these fundamental defects. As for himself, he had no desire whatever to engage in love-making. The female sex was the sworn enemy of reason. It was only because the ladies often had lively minds that it was amusing to come to them with unshakeably logical arguments and to watch how they applied their sophisms and prejudices to these.[29]

In spite of these protestations, Joseph was not able to do without women entirely. The always active Viennese gossips reported that an intimate rendezvous was arranged with this or that Court beauty. Sometimes these stories even corresponded to the facts. But these encounters were never anything but the briefest adventures. These ladies of the Court, who would have liked nothing better than an amorous interlude with their supposedly inaccessible Emperor, were most often driven away by his drawn-out and awkward silences, relieved only by ill-timed ironic sallies.[30] In all probability he was only trying to mask his shyness, but every woman wants to have the satisfaction of being courted at least perfunctorily, even by the All-Highest. His successes were not notable, which only reinforced his misogyny. As he was still a young man who could not well do without sexual release, he fell into the habit of letting his valet arrange brief amorous passages for him. As he admitted to Leopold, these were with ordinary women of the streets. Never mind, they served the purpose. Later on he entered into a more permanent arrangement with his gardener's daughter, whom he would visit for a brief quarter hour most evenings. None of this was very elevating, nor could it have been satisfactory.

To complicate matters, Joseph fell in love again. The lady was the Princess Eleanor of Lichtenstein, one of the great beauties of the court. Her physical resemblance to the late Isabella was, if not striking, considerable, and Joseph was not unaware of this. He began to seek out her company, riding beside her carriage in the Prater, drawing her into conversation at official functions. She was, of course, married, but this would have been no obstacle to a liaison, particularly as Eleanor soon fell in love with her attentive courtier. But Joseph apparently was no longer capable of making a simple declaration of his feelings. Having gone to some trouble to arrange to be alone with her at the town palace of his friend, Field Marshal Lacy, he could think of nothing more seductive to say to Eleanor than that he thought of her as he would of his wife: one is not in love with one's wife, but takes a constant interest in everything about her. As any woman of spirit would have been, the Princess was offended and replied that she was quite unable to penetrate into His Majesty's metaphysics. It may be that the role of the constantly rebuffed swain was the one which Joseph wanted for himself. Certainly he now had ample opportunity to play it. The complicated and circumstantial arrangements which he eventually made to further this curious courtship have something psychologically unreal about them. So that he might see Eleanor whenever he wished, yet neither compromise her nor be compromised, he encouraged one of her friends, Princess Kinsky, to entertain Eleanor along with three other princesses, one of them her sister, at the Palais Kinsky almost every evening. These gatherings, soon known as "at the five princesses," were open only to the Emperor and to his friends Lacy and Count Rosenberg. Here Joseph would appear three or four times a week, year in and year out, and converse freely with Eleanor and the other ladies about his various concerns. It was undoubtedly a release for him to be able to shed his necessarily formal manner and to discuss what was worrying him at any given time in this quite informal context, but as a human relationship it left much to be desired.

CHAPTER VI

Joseph's Diplomacy and the "Potato War"

MARIA THERESIA INTENDED THAT JOSEPH SHOULD BE CHIEFLY RE-
sponsible for the military establishment and for the army reforms
which appeared necessary. For these things he had a considerable predilection, but neither talent nor judgment. Although he
thought of himself by preference as a soldier, and always dressed
the part, he was in fact a civilian through and through.

The Austrian army had all but collapsed under the first Prussian attacks in the Silesian wars and its restoration to a degree of
effectiveness had been the work of Maria Theresia's earlier years
in power. In the Seven Years' War the army had performed much
more creditably and had on occasion fought the Prussians to a
standstill. But, on the whole, Frederick had had the better of it,
certainly if one considers the overwhelming continental alliance
he had faced. After the end of the war, informed opinion in Austria held that the army was still not on the Prussian level and that
the only way to improve it was to copy Prussian methods. This
was advice that was welcome to Joseph, and as the Empress in
spite of her dislike of Frederick had the good sense to recognize
that his methods were often effective, it was soon acted upon. Unfortunately it proved a difficult program to carry out.

To begin with, there was a degree of dissension caused by personal jealousies. Unquestionably, the general who had emerged
from the Seven Years' War with the foremost reputation and the
most impressive victories to his credit was Gideon von Laudon.
But after the war the Presidency of the *Hofkriegsrat* was given
not to him but to Franz Moriz Lacy, whose reputation was by no
means the equal of Laudon's but who enjoyed the particular
favor of Maria Theresia and was soon to become the intimate
friend of Joseph.¹ Laudon resented what he considered an un-
merited slight and for some time withdrew to his estates. Later on
the ill feeling generated by this incident was to have a most unfortunate effect on the Austrian army.

More important was the fact that instituting Prussian methods
meant riding roughshod over the interest of all classes. For cen-

turies high military rank had been the exclusive preserve of the high nobility. This now came to an end. Joseph insisted, and Maria Theresia agreed, that ability would have to be the only criterion for promotion. Particularly the practice of installing the seventeen- and eighteen-year-old sons of wealthy and deserving members of the nobility as colonel-proprietors of regiments would have to cease.[2] At any rate, the new service regulations which were laid down tended of themselves to eliminate the military dilettante; officers were expected to exercise their troops or to perform necessary office work for a minimum of nine hours a day. This was no doubt to the good, but involved a period of transition in the officer corps. There would inevitably be a time during which the new men had not as yet accustomed themselves to command and would tread very carefully, particularly as there was no telling when the influence of the great families might reassert itself.

Prussianization also meant overhauling the cumbersome and inefficient machinery used to fill the ranks of the army. This could be done effectively by conscription, which indeed Joseph soon succeeded in introducing, with the exception of the provinces of Hungary, Tyrol, the Austrian Netherlands, and Lombardy. As was the case with eighteenth-century conscription generally, the principal burden of this fell on the peasantry. The landed nobility of course protested on the ground that it was being deprived of its field workers, but Joseph insisted that these complaints be ruthlessly turned back. Still, in practice the local authorities generally worked out a system whereby a man might be inducted into the army, given some training, and then granted an extended leave which allowed him in fact to pursue his previous occupation. Thus, when the Venetian ambassador in 1768 reported that the Austrian army consisted of 200,000 effectives and could immediately take the field in that strength, only the first half of his assertion was accurate.[3]

But perhaps the cardinal defect of the Hapsburg army was the paralyzing lack of confidence, both in themselves and in their superiors, which characterized the officer corps. For this there were numerous reasons, the least of which was the uncertainty introduced by the Emperor's insistence that the officer corps be rigorously professionalized. After all, most officers of high station had been dilettantes only in the narrowly literal sense of the word; they delighted in their work. Soldiering was an honorable pursuit, in many cases the only one for which they were fitted, and many of them were completely devoted to it. It was by no means a subversion of the Emperor's will that the majority of officers promoted because of ability turned out to be high noblemen. In this area they could easily hold their own with any competition. Of much greater consequence were two other deplorable circumstances. First, there was an absolute and justified lack of confidence in the highest leadership. Lacy, ill-tempered, pudgy, as vain as Kaunitz, was a competent military administrator but a bungler in the field, and this was known by all. And although Joseph was still an unknown quantity, his frightfully incompetent handling of troops during maneuvers gave rise to the suspicion that he had inherited his father's military abilities, which as everyone knew had been less than nil. When the Emperor later on was actually to command armies, it turned out that he not only bungled according to the script (as the Austrians say so aptly, *er patzte nach Noten*), ignoring strategic imperatives and immersing himself in details which would much better have been left to a moderately competent noncommissioned officer, but that his nerves were bad. He would panic at the first reverse and would convince himself that only disengagement could save his army. All this was a considerable handicap.

Secondly, after the Thirty Years' War the great victories of the Hapsburg armies had come at the expense of the Turks. Turkish armies, because of their vast numbers and because of the absolute authority wielded by their officers, could be formidable, but they were mostly so badly led and so heterogeneous in composition that they fought far below their potential strength. A reasonably determined and half-way efficient opponent could usually prevail against them, even against considerable odds. Then, beginning in 1740, the Austrian generals had suddenly been faced by Frederick the Great who, in spite of the evident smallness of his total resources, would nevertheless maneuver so swiftly and brilliantly that he could generally appear on the field of battle with a force at least the equal of his opponents. And the Prussians fought hard and well. It was enough to give one pause, and more than one Austrian general at the approach of a Prussian army thought first not of how best to bring about its defeat but rather of how to place himself so that a reverse should not be fatal. The long and only sporadically interrupted series of Austrian defeats, to last until the final collapse of 1918, was caused by complicated and deep-seated factors which far transcended the particular circumstances of Joseph's time. He was to find, just like his successors, that it is extremely difficult to play at the game of great power politics without an effective army. It is just the fact that he was so

successful in other areas that lends a particular irony to his failure to create an effective army.

Foreign affairs, strictly speaking, were not within Joseph's sole
purview under the working terms of the co-regency. But, as Maria
Theresia became increasingly concerned about the effects that his
interventions might have, she encouraged him to concern himself
more with foreign policy, probably on the theory that this area
was less sensitive than the internal balance of the Monarchy. For
his part, Joseph was by no means unwilling to let himself be
shoved in this direction. As he had made clear in his earliest
statements of the policy he intended to follow, his notions of the
greatness of the State did not exclude certain desirable accretions
of territory.

In theory, those responsible for the formulation of foreign policy in the eighteenth century subscribed to the doctrine of the
Balance of Power. The respective power relationships between
states were regarded as more or less sacrosanct. Thus, if a power
succeeded in achieving a substantial gain of territory or influence,
because of disordered conditions on the periphery of Europe, it
was necessary to find a compensating advantage for its immediate
rivals, so that the Balance might not be disturbed. Consequently,
the work of diplomacy at the highest level consisted not only of
gaining advantages for the State, but also of finding possible com-
pensations for precisely those who would be disadvantaged by
such gains and of making these palatable to them. As if this were
not complicated enough, practice no longer quite corresponded
to theory. The great gains achieved first by Prussia, then by Russia, in the teeth of all theory, had brought about a situation
no longer compatible with traditional doctrine. If Frederick the
Great was a man of considerable political insight who was willing
to remain content with what he had already won and wanted
nothing more than to see the crystallization of a new Balance of
Power on the basis of these Prussian gains, this restraint did not
apply to the rulers of Russia. The situation in Eastern Europe
promised to become extremely fluid because of the juxtaposition
of a dynamic Russian expansionism and a debilitated Poland as
well as a woefully disorganized and maladministered Turkish Empire. It would be difficult if not impossible to incorporate the
considerable changes which would inevitably result from this
constellation into the old Balance.

The situation of Austria was even more difficult. The Diplomatic Revolution, with which Kaunitz had hoped to undo the
Prussian victories of the Silesian Wars, and which, it had been

feared in some quarters, might well result in an overcompensation, *i.e.* the complete destruction of Prussia as a power, had not even achieved the first result. At the conclusion of the Seven Years' War, Austria was, as before, faced with a strong and inimical Prussia and supported only nominally or not at all by her supposed ally, France. What her relations with Russia, now ruled by the androcide Catherine, would be was still very much of an enigma. In the absence of an all-German power it was still possible to achieve this or that advantage in Germany. But it was clear that any rectifications of the German situation in favor of Austria would require the support not only of France but also of Russia. This last might have to be paid for by concessions which would permit the Russians to grow past all acceptable bounds.

Kaunitz was undoubtedly aware of this difficulty, but refused to face the issue squarely. He could not sufficiently detach himself from his old policy and from the deep-seated Theresian antipathy for Prussia to advocate a genuine rapprochement with Frederick, the object of which would be to make it possible for Austria to reap a large portion of the bounty which would result from the possible dismemberment of Poland and Turkey. But Kaunitz was too much of a realist to have much faith in a grandiose anti-Prussian alliance with Russia. This, he knew, would alarm not only the French but also the English, and, moreover, he had before him a recent and striking example of Russian reliability in such matters. Being unwilling to opt for either of the alternatives which, although dangerous, promised great results, he contented himself with half-measures and deluded himself into believing that the support of France might yet suffice to bring about a satisfactory reckoning with Prussia.

Joseph was the prisoner of no such illusions. He did not like the French and had never promised himself much from an alliance with them. But he was unable to see the whole picture very clearly. While he was aware of the general directions which Austrian policy might plausibly take and knew that a considerable reorientation was necessary, he did not understand that, in order to be effective, such a shift would have to be basic and would carry along with it far-reaching consequences. He was perfectly willing to move in new directions, but he refused to appreciate that this would involve major commitments. As a result, he was forever supporting projects which, while their successful completion would involve a basic shift in policy, were hardly important enough to justify such exertions, and then abandoning them all too readily when it became clear that they aroused resistance from the other powers. As a further complication, moreover, Joseph in his younger years entertained a strong and undisguised liking for, of all people, Frederick the Great. While he did not really disagree with Maria Theresia's opinion that Frederick was their inexorable enemy, he could not suppress his admiration for the efficient and rational manner in which the Prussian king governed his lands. He wanted to emulate Frederick as well as to measure himself against him, and he conceived the notion that if they could meet for informal and leisurely exchanges of views, they might well settle their differences like gentlemen. Needless to say, such opinions, whatever their bearing on reality might have been, hardly fitted within Kaunitz' scheme of things.

In 1766, when Frederick, who was understandably curious about the new emperor, was to review troops in Silesia at the same time that Joseph would be in Bohemia, he dropped a hint at Vienna that an "accidental" meeting would not displease him in the least.[4] But Kaunitz always disliked those enterprises which he did not himself initiate, and Maria Theresia was worried lest Joseph's head be turned by Frederick's liberal ideas; consequently, a refusal was sent without Joseph having been consulted. When the latter learnt of this, he was bitterly disappointed. Three years later Frederick was again anxious to arrange a meeting. This time there were solid political reasons behind his wish. The Russians, in their self-appointed role of protectors of Orthodoxy, had become involved in Poland, which under Stanislas Poniatovski was showing some belated but alarming signs of life. The Turks had taken advantage of this distraction to attack Russia and Catherine's generals had promptly defeated them on all fronts. It began to look as if the Semiramis of the North would preside alone over the liquidation of the Ottoman Empire. This Frederick could not possibly permit, and as it would be to the distinct disadvantage of Austria as well, he conceived the plan of suggesting to Joseph the possibility of a joint Austro-Prussian demonstration in favor of Turkey, with the codicil that everyone should be compensated in Poland.

The two sovereigns met at Neisse in Silesia in August 1769.[5] Kaunitz had laden Joseph down with a mountain of instructions meant to provide against every gambit which Frederick might employ. He need not have taken so much trouble. The King and the Emperor talked for long hours but confined themselves to generalities which could hardly be considered binding. Frederick was distinctly alarmed at the impression Joseph conveyed. He judged him to be consumed by ambition and said later that Europe would be in flames the day that young man achieved sole power in Austria. He was very careful not to commit himself in any way to him. Joseph, on the other hand, allowed himself to be deceived by Frederick's garrulity. He gained the impression that here was an old man, living in the past, no longer dangerous. He hastened back to Vienna to impart this cheerful intelligence to his mother. She, however, knew better and assured him that they would still have reason to concern themselves with the King of Prussia.

By 1772 the Turkish situation had become critical. One Russian victory followed upon the other and there was reason to believe that Ottoman resistance would soon be at an end. Frederick, notwithstanding the circumstance that he was bound to Russia by a treaty of alliance, insisted upon the necessity of joint Austro-Prussian action. Accordingly, another meeting was arranged with Joseph, this time at Neustadt in Moravia. On this occasion Kaunitz accompanied the Emperor. It soon became clear that the Chancellor considered Joseph to be so much excess baggage. He arranged for him to attend maneuvers and review troops while he talked with Frederick alone. Nor was Kaunitz cowed by Frederick. He talked interminably, brooked no interruptions, and lectured the King on a wide variety of subjects. Frederick did not know whether to be amused or angry with such monstrous presumption. When Kaunitz at last condescended to speak about the real subject of the meeting, he declared out of hand that he could not allow Prussian interference in those matters. Austria would never allow the Russians to dismember Turkey to the extent that they would have a common frontier with Austria, but for this Prussian help was unnecessary. Austrian prestige and influence would be quite sufficient to achieve this end. Frederick left Neustadt in a glum mood.

Joseph did not have reason to be satisfied either. Not only did he resent the insulting cavalier manner in which he had been treated by Kaunitz, but he did not agree with the Chancellor's policy. He saw no reason to support the Turks and would much rather have come to an understanding with the Russians. Returning to Vienna, he urged this policy upon Maria Theresia, but got nowhere. As it happened, events forcibly dragged policy behind them. At the same time that the Russians were defeating the Turks, the Polish situation continued to deteriorate. In order to maintain himself at all, Poniatovski had been forced to make concessions to the most reactionary elements in the Polish Diet. This had brought about a revolt of the peasantry of Eastern Poland, which was overwhelmingly Orthodox. The Russians were supporting this rebellion and were now threatening to engulf Poland as well as Turkey. Frederick's argument that Poland should be dismembered instead of Turkey was gaining in force and immediacy. If there were further delay this might no longer be a possible alternative.

Joseph, excited at the prospect of territorial gain, kept pressing Kaunitz for a decision on what claims might most profitably be advanced. He himself was of the opinion that Belgrade and a large part of Bosnia would best suit them, but he was willing to consider other proposals. Maria Theresia was anxious only to have peace restored. To profit from the troubles of others was, for her, *"agir à la Prussienne."* Even if Belgrade could be acquired, it would have been too dearly bought at the price of the honor and good faith of the Monarchy. The Empress, who could not forget that the Ottomans had refrained from attacking her in her most difficult hours in 1740, was not to be persuaded to repay them in false coin now.[6] This being the case, Joseph was able to persuade her that it was necessary to adhere to Frederick's more and more insistent proposals concerning Poland. On the pretext of maintaining order on the borders of the Monarchy, he caused certain frontier districts in Galicia to be occupied by Austrian troops. This step was presently copied by the Prussians and the First Partition of Poland was launched before it even had been agreed upon by the three powers concerned. In the ensuing negotiations the Austrians took a hard line. But Frederick's gibe that Maria Theresia shed tears for the unfortunate Poles, but the more she cried the more she took, was not entirely merited. Joseph drove her relentlessly. When, somewhat later, the question of a few insignificant districts arose, which might or might not have been included in the part of Poland assigned to Austria, he insisted upon their occupation. When Kaunitz advised caution, Joseph did not hesitate to accuse him of cowardice, which caused the Chancellor to submit his resignation. Maria Theresia succeeded in patching up the quarrel only with the utmost effort. Joseph was pleased with himself. He told Leopold that he saw no reason why they should not acquire Belgrade as well in the next year. It seemed that Frederick's judgment had been an accurate one.

As it happened, however, the international situation was considerably quieted by the Partition of Poland. All three partitioning powers required some time to digest their new acquisitions, and no new opportunity to dismember Turkey arose in the next few years. In consequence, Joseph's next intervention in foreign affairs was in an opposite geographical direction. In spite of his failure to elicit any response to his Bavarian plans on his visit to France in 1774, he did not drop the subject.[7] The Elector Max Joseph, still without legitimate issue, was getting older and it would be well for Austria to be prepared for the day of his death. In addition, his heir, Karl Theodor of the Palatinate, was extremely accessible to Austrian blandishments. This prince had a weakness for the French actresses who appeared in his court theater and in the course of a number of dramatic seasons he had fathered a veritable little army of bastards. As he was also a kindly man, he had so far legitimized no less than seven of the boys. While the resources of the Palatinate might suffice for a theater, they were far from equal to providing suitable establishments for so many young princes. Expenses of this magnitude could be borne only by a great power, and Kaunitz who was well aware of this, dangled the possibility of Imperial employment for his sons in front of Karl Theodor. The Elector was fascinated.

In 1775 Joseph began to take a more assiduous interest in the Bavarian question. He asked a small group, from which he pointedly excluded Kaunitz, to look into the claims which Austria might legitimately advance. Their conclusion was that these claims were sufficient to justify a unilateral occupation of all of Bavaria upon Max Joseph's death without the necessity of any diplomatic preliminaries. There is no telling what might have happened if this course had been followed, but in 1776 Kaunitz was able to persuade Joseph to pin his hopes on the negotiations he had been conducting all along on a lower level with Karl Theodor. These appeared even more promising as the Elector's chief minister, Baron von Beckers, was not only a notorious Austrophile from conviction but also was in great need of the sort of financial favors which it was in the power of the Monarchy to bestow. Formal negotiations were taken up. Bavaria, although backward, economically neglected, and egregiously misgoverned, was a valuable prize. It was not only potentially very rich, but its acquisition would be of immense strategic advantage to Austria. The incorporation of some two million German-speaking subjects into the Monarchy would have a considerable effect as well upon its nature, but that does not seem to have been a major element in Joseph's calculations at the time. At any rate, such a prize was worth giving something up for. The question was what.

Two areas suggested themselves as a possible *quid pro quo*. One was the so-called Anterior Austria, a disparate collection of small principalities in western and southwestern Germany, ancient holdings of the House of Hapsburg, not contiguous to the main territory of the Monarchy and for that reason practically indefensible. The other was the Austrian Netherlands, acquired at the end of the War of the Spanish Succession, rich, productive, but far away, difficult to defend, equally difficult to govern because of their ancient traditions and privileges. Various Austrian officials suggested that the one or the other might well be exchanged for Bavaria, and Kaunitz was not in principle averse to either possibility, although Joseph took exception to the second because the yearly income of the Netherlands was rather above that of all of Bavaria and was potentially much greater if the Dutch could be persuaded to lift the Scheldt Barrier which choked off the splendid port of Antwerp. But in the midst of these discussions, Beckers, their principal advocate on the Palatine side, died. Maria Theresia, who had been lukewarm from the beginning, fearing trouble with Prussia, was now ready to drop the whole thing. Joseph, however, was adamant. Although the new Palatine chief minister, Vieregg, was rather less of an admirer of Austria than his predecessor, he agreed to continue the negotiations. Then suddenly fate played a second trick on the Austrians; the Elector Max Joseph fell ill in December 1777. Although his seventeen physicians agreed on a diagnosis of imaginary illness, it soon turned out that he had a particularly virulent type of smallpox. Before the end of the year he was dead. Now there was no longer any time to negotiate. Maria Theresia again urged Joseph to let the matter drop. So far all attempts to get their French ally to make even a mild declaration of support for their position had been fruitless, and she saw Austria facing Prussia alone in a terrible and bloody war fought in a dubious cause. Again Joseph would not hear of retreat, and he had his way.

Karl Theodor was now threatened with immediate Austrian military occupation of all of Bavaria. Under this pressure he caved in and without further argument signed a convention recognizing, in essence, the minimum Austrian demands. In return for various financial considerations most of Lower Bavaria was turned over to Austria. A later exchange of Upper Bavaria for Anterior Austria and possibly Luxemburg was envisaged in a separate clause. As soon as the Elector's signature reached Vienna, Joseph ordered his troops to occupy Lower Bavaria. He was elated. As he saw it, he had stolen a decisive march. Frederick, presented with a *fait accompli,* might bluster, but he would not risk a war to undo it. Joseph could not have been more mistaken.

The King of Prussia had not fought the Austrians in two desperate wars to allow them the bloodless acquisition of such a prize as even part of Bavaria represented. As he saw it, the Balance of Power would be altered by this, perhaps fatally, in favor of Austria. If for the moment he bided his time, it was only because it was preferable to await the spring before launching a major campaign and because he was still in the dark about the intentions of France. But his protests to Austria had an unmistakably menacing tone, and the Prussian military establishment was hastily put on a war footing.

By the spring of 1778 it had become clear that France would not support Austria, that rather the French government looked upon this accretion of strength by their ally with considerable dismay. Without further ado, Frederick declared war.[8] In view of the fact that this step had been all but a certainty for months, the total lack of Austrian preparation and planning does not speak well either for the quality of the high command or for Joseph's comprehension of military matters. Knowing that the Prussians meant to go to war, the Austrians had thought of nothing better to do than to await passively the invasion of Bohemia and Moravia which in previous wars Frederick had made into his trademark. The King did not disappoint them. But this time he did not conduct operations with his old verve. As usual, his forces advanced in separate columns, but one part of the Prussian army, commanded by Frederick's brother, Prince Henry, allowed itself to be held up by only relatively minor Austrian resistance and did not in time effect a juncture which might well have produced another victory of annihilation on the model of, say, Rossbach. The Austrians, having retreated deep into Bohemia, entrenched themselves behind strongly fortified positions. And Frederick did not seem to have the stomach for an all-out frontal attack. Thus the War of the Bavarian Succession quickly degenerated into a series of desultory skirmishes and forays for supplies which soon acquired the derisive label of the "Potato War." Even so, the King had made his point. Considerable portions of the Monarchy were occupied by the enemy, and the Austrians were quite unable to muster the resources to make an end of this unhappy situation. For Maria Theresia this circumstance was decisive. Without consulting Joseph, she initiated peace negotiations. An armistice was agreed on and eventually, in 1779, a peace treaty was signed at Teschen in Moravia. By its terms the Prussians agreed to evacuate Austrian territory, and the Austrians in turn gave back to the by no means delighted Karl Theodor all of Lower Bavaria with the exception of a small district along the river Inn to which Frederick contemptuously referred as a *pour boire*.

Joseph had professed to be furious when he learned of his mother's unilateral peace overtures. But in fact, he had been at the end of his tether. He had been talking of undertaking desperate measures, harnessing the Monarchy's entire resources to the prosecution of the war, but he knew himself that this was only talk. It was part of his nature to throw down his cards and stalk off in a fit of temper when confronted by stubborn resistance and on the whole he was not unhappy to have been bailed out of a difficult situation without having himself to bear the blame for backing down. It was a pity that the end of the Bavarian affair should have been such a ludicrous fiasco, because this rodomontade concealed the fact that the Monarchy had narrowly missed an acquisition, which with a little better luck might well have been made, and which would undoubtedly have had a profound effect on its whole character. A century later a Monarchy containing the Germans of Bavaria in addition to those of Austria might well have reacted to Slav nationalism in a less paranoid fashion and have been less vulnerable to Magyar pressure.

Joseph did not lose his taste for diplomacy because of the Bavarian experience. Only a year later, in 1780, he was deeply involved in schemes involving Russia. In the wake of her recent victories against the Turks, Catherine had conceived the grandiose scheme of restoring the Byzantine Empire, which of course was nothing more than a bit of flummery meant to lend respectability to a Russian occupation of Constantinople. For such a scheme Austrian and not Prussian support would be essential. In consequence, she let it be known discreetly that she was no longer satisfied with her heretofore Prussophile policy and that she would be delighted to meet the young Emperor. Joseph hastened to accept the invitation. He met Catherine in Mogilev, a little town in southwestern Russia.[9] The two rulers got on so well with each other that they decided to travel to St. Petersburg together. During the course of the journey and afterward in the Russian capital, Catherine's first minister and lover, Prince Potemkin, and the Austrian ambassador, Count Cobenzl, conducted exploratory conversations. But in the end it proved possible only to agree on a treaty in which the Austrians promised not to support Turkey against Russia and the Russians reciprocally agreed not to lend any help to Prussia in a conflict with Austria. It was a meager result and, furthermore, the signing of the treaty was connected

with an unseemly dispute. Catherine, in violation of the custom
by which the Holy Roman Emperor always had precedence and
affixed his name to treaties first, demanded to sign her name
alongside Joseph's. The latter refused to abandon his ancient
right, and in the end the treaty had to be ratified by an exchange
of letters. But in spite of this, Joseph returned from Russia delighted with his visit, full of praise for all he had seen. He was
evidently of the opinion that great diplomatic gains could result
in the future from the cooperation of these two Courts, a judgment which Maria Theresia rejected as outrageous. She was to be
proven only too right.

CHAPTER VII

Sole Ruler

UPON HIS RETURN FROM RUSSIA JOSEPH EXPRESSED A DESIRE TO visit England. Maria Theresia, to whom the English were the incorporation of all Protestant malevolence, urged him not to go. She also complained that his frequent absences were becoming increasingly difficult for her to bear in her old age. Perhaps it was a presentiment. Her health certainly had not been too good. The physical inactivity she had imposed upon herself after the death of her husband coupled with an inclination to overeat had made her so fat that she could no longer get about unassisted. She slept badly and was comfortable only in a sitting position. She would spend entire nights propped up in a chair. She was always too warm and constantly thirsty. To gain a measure of relief she would sit for hours by an open window and drink glass after glass of iced lemonade. Inevitably, in a typically raw Viennese November, she caught a bad cold. At first it was not regarded as grave, but it did not respond to treatment. Then, on her way to mass, the Empress was seized by a fit of choking. Having regained her breath, she insisted on receiving the last sacrament. Thereafter, although the cold symptoms receded, the Empress complained of growing lassitude. She no longer had much feeling in her limbs. As late as the 27th of November Joseph thought that the situation was not critical. In spite of her discomfort, the Empress was at her desk, writing. But on the 28th it became evident that she was dying. Her pulse was irregular, her breath short and laborious. Joseph spent the whole day with her, attending to her needs. From time to time she would pick up a book and read briefly, then they would converse for a while. On the afternoon of November 29, 1780, Maria Theresia, having sunk into an unquiet sleep, drew her last breath.[1]

Joseph, who had been with his mother to the end, emerged from her death chamber weeping unashamedly. Of all the losses he had had to bear, this was in a way the cruelest. He lamented that he had now stopped being a son, the role which he thought he had succeeded in filling best. To be forced to make an end of a

relationship which had lasted for almost forty years, he wrote to
Leopold, was almost more than his reason could bear. He had lost
his wives, his children, his father, and now his mother. He was as
good as done in the world, only his friendship with his brother
was left him.

Joseph's sorrow was undoubtedly genuine. In spite of his frequent clashes with his mother he had been deeply devoted to her,
and on more than one occasion, when his enthusiasms had led
him into a difficult situation, he had depended on her strength
and her healthy intelligence. He had the good sense to know how
much he had lost with her death. Kaunitz also was deeply moved,
Count Philip Cobenzl having been charged with bringing him
the sad news. Cobenzl found Kaunitz entertaining some guests
and stood behind a chair until he caught the Chancellor's eye and
then merely nodded his head gravely. Thereupon, it was said,
Kaunitz, who never allowed anyone's health to be discussed in his
presence, and was not about to make an exception for the Empress, shed a few quiet tears. Only the Viennese populace, concerned with its immediate interest, did not grieve for the dead
Empress. Maria Theresia had not been seen much in public in
her later years. Thus, there had not been many occasions for the
distribution of Imperial largesse. Moreover, she was blamed for a
tax on liquor that had been lately introduced and was immensely
unpopular. As the Empress was driven for the last time through
the streets of Vienna, the people stood in sullen silence. There
were even a few ugly incidents. A handful or two of mud was
thrown at the coffin. It was a sad end for a woman who had with
all her being served her people.[2]

Even if it had suited his temperament, Joseph could not have
given himself up to his grief. There was obviously much work to
be done. Most urgently, the Empress' last wishes had to be carried
out. Her will, it turned out, was a plethora of linguistic and legal
confusion.[3] Joseph despaired of ever making any sense of it, but
he was determined not to interfere in any way in its execution so
that no one might accuse him of meddling. Surprisingly, the larg-
est bequest was a sum to be distributed as a bonus among all her
troops. But, of much more consequence than these immediate
concerns was the fact that after some fifteen years of frustration
Joseph was now in possession of the sole power. A great deal was
expected from him by all those who were to some extent aware of
his inclinations. Frederick the Great proclaimed that a new order
of things was about to begin. Of course, he was probably thinking
of foreign affairs. He had already had one unpleasant experience

with the impetuous Joseph and now feared for the Balance of
Power. But such literary figures as Herder, Klopstock, and Wie-
land hastened to publish verses in which they greeted the new
order. The last named, perhaps the most gifted and surely the
most liberally inclined of the leading German writers of the
eighteenth century, wrote that fortune had chosen Joseph to create a better world. Goethe wrote that according to reports reaching him from Vienna the Viennese had greeted Joseph's accession
in the manner of sun-worshipers celebrating the appearance of
the heavenly orb.[4] Whether the Emperor would in fact fulfill all
the liberal dreams which were beginning to be dreamt even in
German-speaking Europe, remained to be seen. For the time
being however, what was most remarkable about the transition
from Maria Theresia to Joseph was that it was all but impercep-
tible. At first, almost nothing happened.

Joseph asked Kaunitz to remain at his post, and the Prince hastened to reply that he would continue to serve him with all the
zeal at his command.[5] Along with the Chancellor all the other
leading department heads were retained, at least for the present.
Joseph wrote Leopold that their mother's death had created
enough confusion already. He would for the nonce let everything
go on on its accustomed fashion and slowly prepare people's
minds for the changes which for so long a time he had considered
necessary. This was good advice which the Emperor gave himself,
and he did not ignore it. He was, moreover, tired, depressed, and
sick. A December in which the penetratingly cold rains refused to
turn to snow was not a propitious time to embark on great projects. The state continued to be administered much as it had been
and it happened that the first to feel the effects of the changing of
the guard were the members of the Imperial family. Here there
were no tactical considerations which imposed a lack of celerity
upon the Emperor and he proceeded to effect some changes he
had long desired. In his opinion the inner Court circle in his
mother's last years had become a monstrous regimen of women.
Joseph, whose need for exclusively female companionship was already well served at the five princesses', hastened to exile his un-
married sisters to the convents of which they had heretofore been
only the nominal abbesses. He also insisted on the introduction of
various and not so small economies. The exceedingly generous
allowances to members of the family were cut appreciably if not
radically. Once again, just as at the time of his accession as co-
regent, the expenses of the Court were reduced. A great many
rooms in the Hofburg which were never used, were closed off.

Servants were let go, horses were sold, the number of courses
served at State dinners was reduced.[6] Joseph's instructions for the
conservation of funds were detailed and in some aspects really
petty, being an interesting foretaste of an aberration which later
would mar many of his more significant actions.

Two events which are directly connected with the death of
Maria Theresia had a portentous character. The new Pope, Pius
VI, refused the Empress the special papal service for deceased
monarchs, on the ground that it was not the custom to accord it
to women. The papal legate in Vienna protested against this decision, but the Pope chose to reply that he did not care in the
least what the Emperor thought of his decision. Thereupon Joseph wrote, in his own hand, as a footnote on an official document
addressed to the Roman Curia, that it was all the same to him
whether the Bishop of Rome was well- or ill-bred.[7] There the
matter rested, but Pius was to hear of it again. Then, the Hungarian Diet approached Joseph with the humble reminder that it
was necessary for the new Monarch to be crowned in Hungary
and to take an oath of loyalty to the Hungarian constitution.
Joseph, who had no wish to be bound in this way, gave an evasive
but conciliatory answer, which the Hungarians interpreted as an
assurance that he did not intend to interfere in a basic sense with
their traditional relationship to the Monarchy. This misunder-
standing was to be the cause of much friction later on.

In order to curb his impatience to begin work on the reform
program which he had postponed some time before, Joseph early
in 1781 undertook yet another journey, this time to the Austrian
Netherlands and to France. In Brussels Joseph spent his time
assisting at the meetings of various administrative bodies and
courts. The fabulous multiplicity of institutions which characterized the Netherlands was anything but pleasing to him and he
despaired of ever introducing any meaningful order there.[8] Once
again, as in 1778, his thoughts turned to the possibility of ex-
changing these rich, but as seen from Vienna, anomalous provinces. In Paris the Emperor devoted himself to repairing the
breach which had appeared in the French alliance at the time of
the war over Bavaria. He was charming, his hosts were infinitely
polite, and perhaps he deluded himself into believing that he had
succeeded in allaying the deep suspicions with which the policies
of Austria were regarded at Versailles. Unlike the occasion of his
previous visit, he did not appear in public and he left no record
of what his impressions of the state of the French monarchy were,
beyond the comment that he was favorably impressed with the

celebrated fictitious budget which the minister of finance, Necker, had recently published.[9] But Joseph's mind was quite evidently not on what he was doing. He was impatient to return to his capital, to begin the work of reshaping the State, a task which he had only so recently deliberately postponed. By August he was back in Vienna, but he did not have the patience to stay there, either. Within a few days he was inspecting troops in Bohemia, then in Hungary, then in Italy. It seemed for a time that he wanted to be everywhere at once. Perhaps this was purely delight at seeing at first hand all the facets of what was now solely his, or he might already then have been driven by the conviction that there was an infinity of work to be done and perhaps not much time to do it.

While the Emperor was dashing about his provinces, the *Staatsrath,* duly instructed by him, was beginning to address itself to the question of reform. Cogently enough, Joseph was of the opinion that, like charity, reform ought to begin at home. Before it would be possible to introduce significant changes into his dominions, it would be necessary to change the administrative apparatus which would be in charge of working out and implementing these changes. To say that the Austrian administration at Joseph's accession was ponderous would be an understatement. The principle that the authority of the provincial estates was subject to the authority of the Court had been established beyond recall by Leopold I in the previous century and had been reinforced under Maria Theresia, but in spite of repeated efforts the late Empress had not been able to make the central authority into an efficient instrument of government. At her death there were no less than 1,500 court chamberlains, each of whom could advance a claim to administrative responsibility in some area. This horde of officials was the result of a system which demanded of each new chamberlain, upon his nomination, the payment of a considerable sum to the Lord Chamberlain. That official was of course interested in seeing to it that as many new offices were created as possible. Understandably, the chamberlains for the most part attempted to recover their investment by concerning themselves with their *ressorts,* at least to the point where some money might be extracted from them.[10] All this vitiated, to a point, Maria Theresia's attempts to define spheres of administrative responsibility, of which the creation of the *Staatsrath* had been only one.

Joseph had little patience with useless officials who "sat endlessly on their behinds and produced redundant copies of everything." [11] He let it be known that henceforth it would be not only the right but the duty of every department head to confer with him, in any costume, at any hour, if there was a pressing problem to discuss. He hoped that out of those frequent conferences the officials would eventually emerge with a complete familiarity with his thought processes and would, thereafter, be able to make decisions entirely in the spirit in which he wished them made. Conduct lists, on which department heads were to evaluate the performance of their subordinates, were introduced.[12] It was objected that this was a waste of time because no official would wish to draw unfavorable attention to himself by criticizing his own department, but these objections overlooked the inherently vicious nature of every bureaucracy. The department heads were only too glad to justify their varied failures by blaming those below them, and ultimately the conduct lists became one of the most feared aspects of Josephinian Austria. Still, in view of Joseph's earlier frequent and unrestrained attacks upon the hopeless inefficiency of Austrian officialdom, very little in the way of fundamental change was introduced. Not until the High Chancellor, Count Blümegen, was caught in an unsavory business involving both peculation and nepotism, and was dismissed, were there any significant changes in personnel and even then their number was limited.[13] For the most part the Emperor contented himself with retaining the officials he had inherited, including the superfluous ones, and exhorted them ceaselessly to perform their duties more conscientiously. As late as 1783, in his so-called "pastoral letter," he complained that he was being everywhere badly served and reminded his officials that "he who wishes to serve the State must think of himself last . . . only one intention can guide his actions, the greatest good for the greatest number." This last excursion into Benthamite rhetoric should not obscure the fact that Joseph's work was done with very imperfect instruments. The wholesale dismissals of which he may have once dreamt would have had a crippling effect on the State, and were, moreover, quite unnecessary. It soon turned out that useful work could be gotten out of a substantial number of heretofore donothing officials, once these had become convinced that the Emperor's attention was riveted on them.

This raises the question of the participation of the nobility in Joseph's reform program. As will presently be seen, many of his measures were evidently directed against the ancient privileges of that class and he did not hesitate to make the most caustic remarks about the inefficiency of nobly born ne'er-do-wells. Also,

the Emperor showed a distinct preference for giving employment
to able members of the middle classes. Sonnenfels is only the best
known of these, there were many others. No less than seven cabi-
net secretaries, a position just below that of minister, were of non-
noble origin, and it has been estimated that seventy-five percent
of the government officials employed in Vienna under Joseph
were not nobles.[14] In spite of this, it would be mistaken to assume
that the Emperor pursued a policy of deliberately excluding the
aristocracy from high office. It should not be overlooked that
the greater part of his most influential ministers were not only
nobles, but members of the old and caste-bound Court aristocracy. Under Joseph government careers might have begun to be
open to the talents, but a talent unfolding in a gentleman of
quality was still at an advantage. Nor was this the result of un-
conscious forces, or of the weight of tradition prevailing in the
face of an insufficiently prepared attack upon it. Joseph deliberately meant to make use of the aristocracy in the governing of the
State. Far from wanting to abolish it, he saw it as the class which,
once it had been accustomed to strict obedience and long hours,
would be the Crown's first and most reliable servant. Undoubtedly, the example Joseph had before him was Frederician Prussia.
It was not a really meaningful comparison because of the great
differences between the Prussian and Austrian states. But a comparison between Joseph and Louis XIV is not nearly as absurd as
might appear at first glance. Just as the Sun King could build
upon the foundations laid by Richelieu and Mazarin, Joseph had
the advantage of being able to proceed from a starting point beyond the cameralist reforms beginning with the reign of Leopold
I and culminating in that of Maria Theresia. And the role which
the Emperor wished the nobility to play was considerably less
negative than that which is traditionally associated with Versailles. It might not prove possible to transform the Austrian aristocracy into a higher civil service on the Prussian model, a clan
whose members judged themselves in terms of how high a position they had achieved in the service of the Crown, but they were
not meant to be mere *féneants,* either.

The one administrative area in which a thoroughgoing upheaval, both of policy and of personnel, took place was the police
force. In February 1782 Count J. A. von Pergen was appointed
Regierungspresident of Lower Austria, a position which corresponded to that of chief of police for Vienna. It was Joseph's
intention from the beginning that Pergen should be more than
merely the principal keeper of order in the capital. Joseph

wanted him to create what was essentially a secret police, not too
different from that institution as it has become all too fulsomely
known in the modern totalitarian state. There was no lack of
example for Pergen to follow. Under Maria Theresia there had
been a morals police (*Sittenpolizei*) which kept a sharp lookout
for any evidence of immoral behavior or of overt criticism of the
government. An indiscreetly conducted flirtation or a chance remark could mean serious trouble with the authorities. As the Emperor conceived it, Pergen's police force was not to engage in
petty spying upon the population. It was, rather, to have a more
positive function. It was intended to serve as an instrument which
would permit Joseph to be informed exactly about the extent to
which the problems of the Monarchy were being attended to and,
conversely, to assure that all his servants were constantly apprised
of his intentions and wishes. For a time, contrary to the expectations of the cynics, Pergen's organization actually conformed to
this, to put it mildly, idealistic premise. There is no doubt that
Vienna, in the early years of Joseph's reign, had the reputation of
being one of the freest cities in Europe. The Viennese, always
known as complainers, gave free rein to their natural inclinations
and did not spare a single aspect of Joseph's administration with
their criticisms. When a particularly nasty attack was reported to
him, his answer was that he was perfectly willing to let anyone say
whatever he pleased, so long as he, in turn, was permitted to do as
he wished. But ultimately Joseph was to lose sight of his intention
to forbear, and the natural tendency of any organization pro-
tected by secrecy and invested with power to behave in an arbitrary and autocratic manner gained the upper hand. Pergen's police began to collect, actually to solicit denunciations, and was for
some years the terror of Austrian officialdom. This unhappy circumstance is only partially mitigated by the undoubtedly true
assertion that Joseph had at long last lost patience with the dila-
tory, inefficient, careless ways, the *Schlamperei* inherent in Austrian officialdom, and was determined to light a fire under it.

If increased efficiency in the administrative apparatus was Joseph's first concern, the necessity for some sort of standardization
was not far behind. In spite of the best efforts of nearly a century
of cameralism, the Austrian Monarchy could still not belie its
somewhat unusual genesis. It had grown over the centuries, almost haphazardly, as the result of marriages, deaths, wars, chance
alliances, and Turkish pressure upon Eastern Europe, and it possessed less of the unified character resulting from ancient and
common traditions than any other European state, saving per-

haps the Ottoman Empire. Although the political independence
of the various provinces had been greatly reduced, their heterogeneous nature persisted just below the surface of obedience to high
policy decisions. Every attempt to enforce any measure equally in
the whole Monarchy was met with foot-dragging, obstructionism,
or even open resistance in at least a part of the country. Before
long it had become clear to Joseph that unless he found a way to
overcome the necessity for enforcing his decisions separately in all
his dominions, all his energies would soon be expended on this
problem alone.

In order to further what he considered a necessary work of cen-
tralization, Joseph decided that it would be well to begin by
eliminating the Babel of linguistic confusion which prevailed in
the Monarchy. A common administrative language would have to
be introduced. In this he was guided solely by considerations of
utility. While he ultimately settled upon German, he first considered Czech, which he rejected only because he convinced himself
that the forcible introduction of a Slavic language would cause
too much unrest among the Magyars. Thus the accusations lev-
eled against him by some of his enemies that he intended to Ger-
manize his dominions are quite without foundation. But once he
had decided upon the introduction of German, he proceeded
with an insistence and an urgency which had already become
characteristic of him. All State business was to be transacted in
German, all government officials were to demonstrate a profi-
ciency in that language within, at the most, three years. Most of
the non-German-speaking provinces accepted this decision, some
with better grace than others, but Hungary reacted with a storm
of protest. This was not so much because Hungarian national
feelings were more highly developed, but rather because Hungary, until quite recently a frontier district in large part occupied
by the Turks, was not as accustomed to unquestioning obedience
as other lands with a less disturbed past; and because, in contrast
to the rest of the Monarchy, most officials in Hungary did not, in
fact, speak German and a real hardship would be worked on
them by the Emperor's order. For reasons too complex to go into
here, the administrative language of Hungary was Latin, which
all the officials spoke, although in truth almost without exception
badly. They also, of course, knew Hungarian, although if they
belonged to the high nobility their command of their native language was apt to be sketchy, in which case, however, they spoke
French. Of German, there was hardly a trace. Joseph, however,

turned a deaf ear to all complaints. The Magyar officials could learn German or make room for those who would.[15]

The Hungarians, already deeply offended by the removal of their national relic, the Holy Crown of St. Stephen, from the fortress of Poszony (Pressburg) to Vienna, became convinced that Joseph was their pityless enemy. If they could not oppose him effectively at the moment, their day would come. In their judgment of Joseph, they were, however, mistaken. He had nothing whatever against the Hungarians and was concerned only, as we have noted, with making the government of the Monarchy more efficient. For instance, on the other side of the ledger he insisted that the governments of Transylvania and, later, of Croatia no longer function as separate entities reporting directly to Vienna, but that they deal with the capital through the intermediacy of the government of Hungary only; this was to be of inestimable financial and political advantage to the Magyars. Joseph moved the capital of Hungary from the peripherally located and impoverished Poszony to Buda, thus providing Hungary with a viable political center, but this measure too was resented as an affront to tradition.

With the exception of Hungary, however, Joseph's attempts to centralize the administration were eminently successful. Here, after all, he was building on a solid foundation. By the time of his accession, the position of the monarch had become sufficiently exalted so that it was not to be supposed that the antiquated and jejune feudal institutions of his dominions would offer serious resistance to a frontal assault. The difficulty was rather that, in part because of his deep, almost impulsive commitment to all the varied aspects of his complex responsibilities, in part because of his by no means unjustified suspicion that only that would succeed which he undertook himself, he tried to concern himself with far too much. He was, of course, not alone in this. His contemporaries, Frederick and Catherine, also attempted to gather in their hands all the important threads in the fabric of the State. But Prussia was much smaller, and Russia had an ancient tradition of oriental despotism. In both these countries the monarch could convince himself that he was aware of the fall of the least sparrow, that his will was everywhere done. And, on the surface at least, this was the case. In Austria it was a different matter. Not only were the problems of government more complex because of the nature of the country, but below the level of conformity to political decisions, there was serious and determined opposition to fundamental social or economic change. The nobility, in particular, had acquiesced to the usurpation of its political privileges by the Monarchy only on condition that it was left to do pretty much as it pleased in other spheres. It would be exceedingly difficult to overcome this resistance, and it was to be Joseph's tragedy that only his immediate involvement in a question could achieve any results at all and that his at any rate not particularly robust health would all too soon be broken by these protean demands.

CHAPTER VIII

Judicial Reforms and Censorship

ONE OF THE FIRST SECTORS OF PUBLIC LIFE WHICH JOSEPH DECIDED
to overhaul was the administration of justice. Here, Austrian
practice still lagged far behind contemporary theory, and although Maria Theresia had brought about many improvements,
Austrian justice was still for the most part what it had been before her reign, "expensive to administer, capricious, slow and not
only without mercy but actually cruel." [1] Judicial institutions
everywhere are remarkably resistant to social change and the
Nemesis Theresiana did not constitute a thorough change at that.
Joseph was not only concerned with removing what he considered
a relic of the gray Middle Ages, but he wanted above all to speed
up the judicial process. He was of the not unreasonable opinion
that in order to be effective punishment must follow upon the
crime surely and swiftly. Here too he was motivated perhaps more
by considerations of efficiency than by feelings of humanity, although the end result might have been humanitarian. To be
sure, his first steps in the direction of judicial reform were made
necessary by a simple omission of his mother's and were in reality nothing more than a further assertion of the royal power vis-à-
vis the nobility. Maria Theresia had intended to reform not only
the criminal code but also the civil, under which lesser criminal
offenses were punishable as well. The commission which had been
charged with submitting proposals to this purpose had, after la-
boring for a decade and a half, produced a compilation encom-
passing eight fat folio volumes. It was evident that a new genera-
tion of lawyers would have to devote themselves to nothing but
mastering the intricacies of this compilation, and Kaunitz, in despair, finally advised the Empress to reject these proposals in their
entirety. The result was that the administration of the civil code
remained in the hands of the provincial nobility, which may have
been precisely what the members of the commission had intended.

Joseph was not unaware of these difficulties, but he decided to
cut this particular knot by promulgating a new law code *jure*

regio, that is, without having consulted the Estates. This law code was promulgated in September 1781.[2] More importantly, he did not attempt to produce a whole new code on short notice, but merely decreed that henceforth the jurisdiction of the manorial courts would be drastically limited. They were no longer permitted to impose any fines, and prison sentences of more than eight days were to be subject to review by higher authority. The landowners were required to appoint university trained judges to preside over their courts or to be able themselves to pass the appropriate examinations. All lawyers had to be in possession of doctoral degrees and had to pass a bar examination administered by the Court of Appeals. Once they had accomplished this, they were empowered to plead before any duly constituted court of law, not just the one to which they were accredited.[3] The hope was that in spite of the continued absence of a standardized civil code, a procedural standardization would ensue and would achieve much the same effect. By and large this expectation was fulfilled.

As the years passed, Joseph decided that further steps were necessary. He convinced himself that the degree to which jurisprudence, in spite of the code of 1781, remained in the hands of private persons was dangerous and that the criminal code in particular was in need of modernization. In 1784 he once again appointed a commission to address itself to this problem. This body, working under his constant prodding, produced appreciable results within only three years' time. So far as the administration of justice went, the work of the commission resulted in the decree of August 1787. Only agents of the Crown were to be empowered to make decisions affecting the lives and the freedom of its subjects. And no subject would henceforth be immune from the jurisdiction of the royal courts. The only advantage which the members of the privileged orders retained was that the appropriate provincial estates were notified of any proceedings against a nobleman, and the ecclesiastical authorities of those against a cleric. All judges without exception would now have to be graduates of the faculty of law of a university and had to serve an apprenticeship of several years' duration. In order to immunize the judicial profession against the temptations of bribery, salaries were substantially increased. That of a presiding judge, for instance, was raised from 600 to no less than 3,000 gulden yearly.[4] Thus was laid the basis for the highly professional and proverbially incorruptible judiciary which was to become the pride of the Austrian Monarchy.

The deliberations of the commission of 1784 also produced a general reform of criminal law, the so-called *Allgemeines Gesetzbuch* of January 1787.[5] This code, which bore the stamp of Martini, and to a lesser degree that of Sonnenfels, proceeded from three major premises. The first, a belated borrowing from English legal doctrine, was that no crime could be committed without evil intent. Thus, idiots, children under twelve, and the mentally ill could no longer be prosecuted, since they were adjudged not to be able to distinguish between right and wrong. The second was that every crime committed was a crime against the State and not merely against the individual who was wronged by it. Neither injured parties nor judges were to be allowed the latitude of dropping charges merely because they so wished. If the prosecuting attorney had enough evidence to the effect that a crime had been committed, judicial proceedings were mandatory. Thirdly, equality before the law was established. Or rather, there was a full turn of the wheel. Where previously noble birth, if it did not accord an accused immunity from prosecution, had at least given him the certainty of privileged treatment in the courts, it was now to be considered an aggravating circumstance. Someone who had enjoyed the advantages of good breeding and high social position was all the more to be blamed if he gave way to his lower instincts. But, in no case were the dependents of a convicted criminal to be included in his punishment.

There was a perceptible shift in the categories of crime which were to be prosecuted with particular vigor. Treason and rebellion were especially emphasized. It now sufficed for small groups of citizens to offer even casual resistance to any officials of the State to produce a capital charge. In contrast, libel and slander were not punished with any particular severity. Joseph, who was for the most part indifferent to the lampoons and canards which circulated about him, probably felt that if it were permissible to denigrate the Emperor, others should not be more sensitive. Black magic, witchcraft, and heresy were dropped from the calendar of crimes and were to be punishable only as ordinary swindles. But procurement, which had flourished in Vienna and had enjoyed the enthusiastic patronage of the high nobility, was to be punished by a year in jail, fifty strokes, and exhibition in the stocks. Moreover, the customers were to be placed under house arrest. Another anachronism out of the Middle Ages was disposed of with the dropping of the formal prohibitions against usury. The lending of money at interest, which of course was an established practice, now became legal and was thus subject to official regulation. A maximum rate of 6 percent per annum was set. The stain of dishonor which had formerly been attached to "fallen women," that is, those ladies of whom it was known that they at one time had engaged in an extra-marital relationship, was removed, and it was no longer permitted to place obstacles in the way of their subsequent marriage. Illegitimacy was no longer to be a legal concept and all disabilities which had heretofore arisen therefrom were removed.[6] But an entirely new crime was discovered. Suicide, which previously had been subject only to condemnation by the Church, was now to be punished with the greatest severity. To be sure, those who succeeded in taking their lives were beyond the vengeance of the courts, but their bodies were to be dragged through the streets by the hangman and then thrown into a pit. Unsuccessful suicides were to be jailed until they had come to realize that self-preservation was a duty toward God, the state, and oneself. There is little doubt that Joseph, to whose personal intervention this measure was due, was most concerned with the second of these duties. He did not intend to be robbed of subjects who for one reason or another found themselves in personal difficulties.

In the matter of punishment there were considerable changes as well. Sonnenfels had been agitating for the abolition of the death penalty for a good fifteen years. Even during the co-regency he had so far convinced Joseph that the latter had agreed in principle that it should be applied only in extreme cases. That was as far as the Emperor was willing to go at this time. Capital punishment was, in theory, retained. Death sentences were pronounced, the judgment was read to the condemned men, but except for the presence of peculiarly aggravating circumstances, they were committed to life imprisonment. In actual fact, only one execution took place in Austria in Joseph's reign, and he removed the chief justice of a Hungarian district because he obstinately persisted in carrying out death sentences. But this does not mean that the Emperor was giving way to pity for poor transgressors. Rather, he was of the opinion that a lifetime at hard labor under nearly inhuman conditions was a more effective deterrent to crime. Men convicted of serious offenses were set to dragging barges up the Danube, they slept in the open on the hard ground and were generally far from coddled. In one year, out of forty-six such maximum security prisoners, twenty died. Even those who had committed lesser offenses were not to be allowed to laze away their days behind bars. They went about at all times in chains and were frequently brought out to perform humiliating tasks in public, such as sweeping the streets of Vienna. In certain cases the punishments permissible under the old laws were even increased in their severity. The branding of certain classes of offenders, a practice which Joseph insisted be retained, was henceforth to be carried out in public. The number of blows with a cane to which a miscreant could be condemned was increased from fifty to a hundred. Interestingly, fines disappeared completely from the register of punishments, as Joseph reasoned that they were not really a deterrent to the rich and that for the poor they meant ruin.

In 1788 some additional regulations were laid down.[7] These emphasized the duty of each citizen to denounce any crime of which he was aware. Only husbands, wives, and near relations were exempt from the necessity of denouncing one another. Once a denunciation was made, an arrest followed, and the prisoner was subjected to a preliminary interrogation. During this he was not to be physically harmed, threatened, or tricked. If he confessed at this point, his guilt was considered established and no trial was necessary. If he did not, he was turned over to a *Strafgericht,* or court of first instance. The accused was still not to be harmed, except that if he refused to answer questions during the proceedings he could be beaten until he did. The accused was not, however, allowed benefit of counsel. The court considered proof of guilt to be either a confession at this point or the testimony of two witnesses who were not *a priori* inimical to the accused. If he was convicted, he had the right to appeal to a higher instance, in the last resort to the Monarch himself. The appeal could be drawn up by a lawyer. If convicted, the prisoner himself had to pay the costs of his imprisonment, or if appropriate, the fee of the public hangman, at the rate of fifteen gulden for execution, ten for branding, and one for a caning.

There were other important legal innovations. Marriage was declared to be a civil contract, and the courts were to have the authority to grant divorces in cases where the bishops refused.[8] As was to be expected, the clergy protested sharply, but Joseph paid no heed. Primogeniture, with the exception of certain few large estates, was abolished, and a man now had the right to leave his property to anyone he wished. Dueling, which the Emperor regarded not only as a barbarous medieval relic but also as a stupid waste of man power, was strictly forbidden. The nobility was considerably upset by these last two edicts, but their protests availed them no more than those of the clergy. The last remnants of torture which had survived the reforms of the 1770s were done away with; only whipping, branding, and exposure in the stocks were retained, and those as strictly regulated punishments.

While Joseph's judicial reforms were considerable, it would be an exaggeration to speak of him as a great lawgiver. Much of the work had already been begun under Maria Theresia, and much of it was limited even by the standards of the time. Although he, in effect, abolished the death penalty, the conditions of prisoners pulling barges on the Danube or, even worse, being galley slaves on old derelict men-of-war tied up on the river, amounted to a living death. And the absence of defense by counsel in criminal proceedings continued to deprive defendants of a right which had already become established in most of the countries of Western Europe.

In the closely allied area of censorship and the liberty of the press, Joseph, who had already in his mother's lifetime agitated constantly for liberalization, began his reign with a sweeping reform. He was convinced that Maria Theresia had made herself ridiculous by forbidding the circulation of works which elsewhere had become established classics and by going so far as confiscating the libraries of foreign diplomats at the frontier. He was enough of a child of the Enlightenment to believe that some salutary changes could be brought about by the free circulation of new ideas and he was also so much of an eighteenth-century autocrat that the notion that his own position might be weakened thereby never occurred to him at all. In 1781 he removed from the ecclesiastical authorities all further responsibility for censorship and placed it in the hands of a newly created commission under the directorship of a man with the reputation of an enlightened thinker, Count Chotek. The poet and ex-Jesuit Blumauer, who had frequently been in trouble because of his outspoken anti-clerical views, was appointed chief censor.[9] Joseph's instructions to the commission were to forbid only such works which were couched in outrageous language or which were unmistakable attacks on Christian morals, on the Church, or on Imperial authority. As for the rest, there was no need to fear criticism. If such a work were to prove false, it would collapse of itself; if true, the state would profit from it. As was to be expected, the lifting of the barriers was followed by the publication of a flood of pamphlets, many of them scurrilous attacks on the person of the Emperor. Practically every measure of his was greeted with a new wave of published criticism. Joseph, true to his announced principles, refused to lose his equanimity over this, although he read many of these attacks carefully. When such an attack struck him as justified or well taken, he would invite its author to visit him and to expand upon his strictures in conversation. If the man made a convincing impression, he was apt to be rewarded with a gift or an offer of employment. Nor was this an attempt by the Emperor to buy off his critics. He was merely of the opinion that efficiency should be rewarded, even if it consisted in proving him wrong.

Of the works which had been hitherto forbidden, the most prominent to remain on the proscribed list were the complete works of Voltaire. There was much in them which offended even Joseph, and as we have already seen, the Emperor had something of an antipathy for the sage of Fernay, perhaps ultimately also because of the latter's close association with Frederick the Great. But, if Joseph had hoped that the liberalization of the censorship, after the first rush of *furor scribendi* had spent itself, would result in the birth of an Austrian literary school of the first rank, he was to be disappointed. The serious literature produced by such people as the chief censor himself, and by Johann Pezzl, never surpassed the meretricious and the mediocre. And the eruption of abysmal junk refused to abate. It speaks volumes for Joseph's forbearance that he even permitted the publication of a pamphlet entitled *The Forty-Two-Year-Old Ape,* which, as it happened, appeared in his forty-second year.[10] At last, however, it became evident that a halt would have to be called. In 1784 it was decreed that every author would have to deposit the sum of six ducats at the time a manuscript was submitted to the censor. If the censor refused permission to print, the money was to be forfeited to poor relief. This measure resulted in a perceptible diminution of pamphlets, not so much because the censor proceeded with increased severity, but rather because many authors were unable to produce the six ducats in the first place.

The censorship affecting the production of plays in Vienna was not very severely administered, either. In Joseph's reign only one work, which was manifestly lascivious, was turned down by the censor, but here another factor was at work. Play production was expensive and private companies did not flourish in eighteenth-century Austria. For all practical purposes the court theater, the famous Burgtheater, enjoyed a monopoly in the capital. Thus the management of the Burgtheater could, by refusing to put on a certain play, exercise a censorship of its own. *Die Räuber* by Schiller was not put on, nor was Beaumarchais' *The Marriage of Figaro.* A play by a certain Grossmann was rejected because it mercilessly satirized the nobility, and a work entitled *Lucinde,* in which Joseph was praised to the skies for his anti-clerical policies, also was not produced.[11] The Emperor's guiding principle was that he did not wish to see the stage transformed into a platform for the dissemination of political views, no matter whether they were favorable or unfavorable to him.

It has already been noted that during the co-regency Joseph took a lively interest in education. This continued to be the case after 1780. His position with reference to pedagogical questions was anything but straightforward. If a certain ambivalence had characterized it earlier, it later became downright paradoxical. The difficulty arose from the circumstance, that although the Emperor as a child of the Enlightenment subscribed to the thesis that an educated subject is much more useful than an illiterate one, he at the same time distrusted most intellectuals. These people, in his opinion, merely devoted themselves to transforming simple questions into complicated ones. For the great majority of his subjects a modicum of education, which would enable them to perform the tasks which life required of them, was more than adequate.[12] The result was that he supported and developed the educational establishment in precisely an inverse ratio to its complexity. As practically everyone would be a more useful servant of the State if he could read, write, and had the rudiments of arithmetic, the elementary schools were not only massively supported, but ultimately made compulsory in all but name. A flood of pamphlets apprised the population of the advantages of schooling, and these were by no means only positive, as illiterates were debarred from entering upon apprenticeship and parents were condignly punished for not sending their children to school by having their school taxes doubled or by being required to perform free labor on school-building projects, depending on their means. Joseph's eagerness to make elementary education universal is explained also by his conviction that the school was the ideal instrument for training his subjects in the eminently desirable qualities of industry, moderation, decency, and godliness, the inculcation of which in the home apparently left something to be desired.

In order to facilitate school attendance, the number of schools was considerably increased; vacations were decreed at harvest time so that the peasants would not be tempted to keep their children out of school altogether for fear that they would not be available when they were needed in the fields; and tuition was not only set very low but was graduated according to the ability of the parents to pay. The rural population paid only one kreutzer a week, the urban two; whoever could produce a certificate of poverty was entirely exempt. Teachers did not have to be paid by the communities but drew their salaries from the central government treasury. Protestants and Jews were allowed to found schools of their own, or if they did not wish to do so, their children were exempted from Catholic religious instruction. The children were to be treated gently and with understanding. There were to be no more than four hours of instruction daily and corporal punishment was to be resorted to only when absolutely necessary. The schools were supplied with free textbooks which were written and printed at government expense. Teachers were not only to be paid decently, but were to be accorded positions of respect in the community. At all official functions they were to be given pride of place after the representatives of the Crown. In view of all this it is hardly surprising that Joseph succeeded in creating a system of elementary education which compared favorably with any other in the world long after his death.

Joseph's efforts in the interest of secondary education were markedly less intense. He realized its importance in the preparation of higher officials, but he was concerned lest the result would be a superabundance of people with more education than they could put to use. Accordingly, tuition was set rather high at twelve gulden yearly, with scholarships available only to the really talented children of the poor. Private academies for the sons of the nobility, even the *Theresianum* to which the Emperor's mother had been so devoted, were closed. The aristocracy could not be prevented from educating its children at home if it wished, but henceforth all house tutors were required to pass the same examination as ordinary secondary school teachers. The curriculum extended over five years and emphasized the study of Latin, mathematics, and German. The teaching of religion, which the Emperor regarded as the best preparation for the responsible performance of important duties, was also given an important place. Corporal punishment was done away with entirely. Secondary teachers were paid rather more than their colleagues in primary education, but they were required to be graduates of a university. The result of these measures was undoubtedly an improvement in the overall quality of the *Gymnasia,* but there was an accompanying reduction in the number of their students. By the end of Joseph's reign there were roughly only half as many pupils attending secondary schools than at its beginning.

The universities were treated by Joseph in what amounted to, at the very least, stepmotherly fashion. As he regarded all education in a pragmatic light and had no use whatever for knowledge for its own sake, there was much about higher education that he regarded as exiguous. The universities were useful insofar as they trained people for the highest positions in the State. But there was only a limited number of such positions open at any given time, and higher education for someone who did not become a State servant was downright damaging, as it did not prepare him to do anything else and merely gave rise to pretentions which prevented him from doing other useful work. This might have been a somewhat narrow view of the nature of a university education, but the Emperor proceeded to act upon it nevertheless. Proceeding from the premise that graduates should be produced only sparingly, he retained only three universities in his domains (Vienna, Louvain, and Pest) and degraded the others to *Gymnasia* with only three-year curricula. In the three remaining universities the emphasis was put on pragmatic subjects, particularly on the faculties of medicine and law. Frills were eliminated, the teaching of foreign languages was practically abolished. The number of professors was greatly reduced, those who remained were not given salary increases that could be compared to those granted to schoolteachers.

It was Joseph's contention that they would be consoled for this inequity by the right which he granted them of being addressed with their titles in civil life. This, incidentally, is a situation which has persisted in the Austrian universities down to the present day. The self-government, even extraterritoriality, which the universities had heretofore enjoyed, was quickly ended and the universities were subjected even in questions of their internal organization to the authority of the State. The influence of the Church over the universities was terminated as well. Professors were relieved of their former obligation to swear an oath to the effect that they believed in the Immaculate Conception. This last helps to explain, at least in part, the Emperor's hostility toward the universities. It was not just that, in his eyes, they were engaged in useless or supererogatory pursuits. They had never succeeded in completely emancipating themselves from the influence of the Counter Reformation, and to him they represented centers of obscurantism and Jesuit inspired opposition to his reform measures. There is no reason to believe that he was entirely wrong about this.

Thus, Joseph can be regarded as the effective creator of a system of primary education which was without its equal in Europe; as at least a furtherer of a more useful system of secondary education; and, if not precisely as an enemy of higher education, at least as a skeptic with regard to it. It is by no means a negative balance.

CHAPTER IX

Religious Reforms

NONE OF THE ACHIEVEMENTS OF JOSEPH II ARE MORE JUSTLY CELE-brated than his accomplishments in regularizing relations between Church and State. We have already noted his categorical opposition to the Jesuits, his defense of the Czech Protestants which he carried to the point of threatening his resignation as co-regent, and his conviction that the Church, like any other institution, was subject to the supreme authority of the State. It was thus only to be expected that he would address himself to these questions without delay, once he had acceded to the sole power. The Pope's petty and uncharitable refusal to permit the celebration of a pontifical mass upon the death of Maria Theresia surely contributed to the Emperor's determination to proceed without undue regard for the sensibilities of Rome. But it should not be supposed that Joseph's fundamental ecclesiastical reforms were in any sense the result of a momentary pique. They were not only the product of many years reflections on his part, but were organically related to certain liberalizing tendencies which had, in spite of the Empress' opposition, characterized the last years of Maria Theresia's reign.

In 1779 and 1780 difficulties with groups of protestants in Moravia had once again arisen.[1] Prince Kaunitz, who ten years earlier had been careful not to associate himself too openly with the cause of religious toleration, availed himself of the occasion to argue from the particular to the general. He bombarded Maria Theresia with a spate of memoranda in which he argued, *inter alia,* that in the absence of the intervention of Divine Grace these Protestants would continue to refuse to be converted to Catholicism, and could they not, in spite of this, be good and useful subjects, and should they not be treated as such? This was an argument whose pragmatic qualities could not fail to appeal to Joseph. When his opinion was elicited he answered that he would be in favor of granting the Moravian Protestants religious freedom provided that the Monarchy be firmly resolved to pay no heed to eventual protests, from whatever side they might come,

and that the same principle of toleration be extended to all the
territories and dominions under his mother's rule. The cat was
now out of the bag: the Emperor, supported by Kaunitz, was pro-
posing nothing less than a general edict of toleration. This was
going too far for Maria Theresia. She might, with considerable
reluctance, have approved some further concessions to her subjects in the Czech territories, about whose constancy in matters of
religion she was at any rate in despair, but a general edict was, as
she explained to Kaunitz, tantamount to a betrayal of her first
and most sacred duty. There the matter rested at the Empress'
death.

With the emergence of Joseph as sole ruler, Kaunitz who in
more recent years had become increasingly identified with the position that the Church must at all costs be subordinated to the
State, no doubt expected that he would now be entrusted with
the realization of a program meant to bring this condition about.
In this he was disappointed. Although Joseph continued to regard him as an indispensable man, the Chancellor had been too
closely identified in other areas with Maria Theresia for the Emperor not to have taken umbrage. There would no longer be a
general deference to the protean wisdom of the Chancellor; for a
time at least he would be restricted once more to pontificating in
the realm of foreign policy. The responsibility for creating the
mechanics of bringing the Church under control, for formulating
a policy to which the rubric *Staatskirchentum* has become attached, was instead turned over to *Hofrath* Franz Joseph
Heinke.[2] Heinke, a one-time student of the German rationalist
philosopher Christian Wolff, had been noticed by Kaunitz soon
after his entering upon State service. In 1769 Heinke had submitted a draft proposal for the reorganization of Church-State
relations which started with the premise that the Church was responsible only for the spiritual welfare of mankind and therefore
could lay no claim to authority in secular matters; it was couched,
however, in so cautiously involute prose that it was possible for
Kaunitz to maintain that it contained nothing disadvantageous
to the Church. Joseph then asked Heinke to submit further proposals, with particular reference to the question of the toleration
of Protestants. Even during his visit to the Netherlands which he
had undertaken principally for the purpose of allowing a hiatus
before attacking the problems of the Monarchy, Joseph could not
restrain himself from deluging Heinke with inquiries.[3] He was
particularly anxious to press for the creation of an Austrian Pa-
triarchate, which he thought would give him more latitude in

dealing with ecclesiastical affairs, but as there seemed to be concerted opposition in the *Staatsrath* to this idea, he let it drop.

At last Heinke's proposal was ready, and after having been thoroughly debated in the *Staatsrath* it was promulgated, essentially without change, in October 1781. This Edict of Toleration decreed that Protestants of the Lutheran or Calvinistic persuasion, as well as members of the Greek Orthodox Church, would henceforth have the right to exercise their religion. A minimum of one hundred families belonging to any of these persuasions in any one district would give them the right to build a church and to hold religious services. However, in order to underline the position of the Catholic Church, which was to remain pre-eminent, these churches were not to have any towers or bells, nor were their entrances to face the street. Protestants were to be given the right to purchase and possess real property, to rise to the level of master in the guilds, and to attain various civil and military dignities. In mixed marriages, the children would become Catholics if that was the religion of the father; if he was a Protestant, the girls would be raised as Catholics, the boys as Protestants.[4]

If this edict did not put the Protestants on exactly the same plane as Catholics, their position now became, certainly by the standards of the day, completely acceptable. Indeed, it turned out that the number of crypto-Protestants had been much greater than generally believed. So many of them took advantage of the newly prevailing conditions and declared themselves that the ecclesiastical authorities professed to believe, perhaps even in good faith, that Joseph's latitudinarianism had resulted in a flood of conversions and that before long he would no longer have any Catholic subjects. The Emperor was convinced at least to the point of establishing January 1, 1783, as the deadline for anyone's changing his official listing from Catholic to Protestant. Those wishing to change their religion thereafter would first have to undergo a six-week course of religious instruction with a Catholic priest. Only if they persisted in their intention at the termination of this period were they allowed to leave the Catholic Church. In actual fact, the number of officially registered Protestants in the whole Monarchy rose to something over 150,000.[5] This might have been, from the point of view of the Catholic Church, a great many, but it certainly in no way threatened its pre-eminent position.

That Joseph was acting more on pragmatic grounds and less from the intellectual conviction that no man could be compelled to believe against his will, can be seen from the limitation of the

Edict to Lutherans and Calvinists. It was to be expected that numerous subjects might be made into more loyal and useful servants of the Monarchy by the toleration of these two major religions. In contrast, the Emperor was absolutely unwilling to tolerate the myriad of small, sometimes insignificant sects which had split off from the main branches of Protestantism.[6] When it was reported to him that a number of families insisted on being registered as Adamites or Deists in the Bohemian religious census, he instructed the officials in charge to give these people two dozen well-aimed blows on their behinds and to send them home, and to repeat the procedure until they cared to identify themselves with one of the major religions.[7]

A special case was that of the Jews.[8] With the annexation of Galicia in the first partition of Poland their number in the Monarchy had more than doubled, having reached 350,000–400,000. Here was evidently a sect large enough to merit inclusion in the pragmatic argument. Immediately upon his accession Joseph did away with the distinctive badge that all the Jews in Austria heretofore had been made to wear (it was re-introduced roughly a century and a half later). He also discontinued the head tax for Jews. In May 1781 he was circulating a draft of a proclamation concerning the Jews which was meant to emancipate them from the disabilities under which they had previously lived; at the same time it was intended to render them "more useful to society at large" by insisting that they learn German and encouraging them to turn to agriculture and various trades in search of their livelihood. There is some reason to believe that the Emperor meant to include the Jews in his Edict of Toleration. But, if that should have been the case, the opposition to his draft proposal was so widespread and vocal, that he soon desisted from this notion. Instead, a series of more limited Toleration Patents were promulgated in various provinces. These still limited the number of Jews who were allowed to settle in any given region and did not permit the erection of public synagogues; they did, however, allow the Jews to send their children to the public schools, to practice trades, to engage in all commercial operations, and to serve in the army. Furthermore, the sumptuary restrictions under which they had labored were abolished. Only Galicia, which was the dwelling place of more than half of the Jews in the Monarchy, was not included in these arrangements. There, the virulently anti-Semetic Polish nobility and gentry had profited from Maria Theresia's pious detestation of the Jews and had been enabled to consolidate an, incidentally extremely profitable, domination over their large Jewish minority. It was not until the very end of Joseph's reign that he was able to introduce a Toleration Patent into Galicia as well.

Since we live in a cynical age, we ought not be surprised that many of the Austrian Jews were anything but pleased with Joseph's efforts on their behalf. Particularly the rabbis suspected that these were nothing but a cunning plot to effect a de-Judaization of their parishioners, chiefly through the instrumentality of the army, which would take in pious Jewish recruits and turn out corrupted soldiers, indistinguishable from gentiles. They addressed outraged protests to the Emperor, demanding that the Patents be withdrawn. It is a sad but well-known fact that a man chained up for a sufficient length of time will come to love his chains. Joseph, for his part, ignored these complaints, as he was in the habit of refusing all protests which emanated from a *parti pris.*

Prince Kaunitz was not the man to accept his virtual exclusion from the conduct of religious affairs without a major effort to recapture the position he had lost. A likely opportunity soon presented itself. The position of the Church in the province of Lombardy, which had only fairly recently come under Austrian rule, was a special one.[9] There the privileges of the Church had not, as in the rest of the Monarchy, been systematically eroded by over two centuries of consistently applied Hapsburg absolutism. The Lombard Church was still financially independent of the Crown and its bishops were nominated by Rome. Kaunitz, under whose purview as Chancellor Lombardy came, had for years been chipping away at this favored position, but without real success. Now he took it upon himself to convince Joseph that this was an anomalous and expensive state of affairs. He was aided considerably in his arguments by the imprudent policy of the Roman Curia, which was not content to let sleeping dogs lie but approached the Austrian Crown with a demand for the preservation and even extension of these privileges. Not only was Joseph persuaded to make an end of them, but Kaunitz succeeded in recapturing for himself at least a part of the responsibility for ecclesiastical matters which had been taken from him. Hereafter there would be a division of authority between the *Staatskanzlei,* where he ruled supreme, and the *Geistliche Hofkommission,* created in 1782 under the direction of Baron Franz Karl von Kressl, whose guiding spirit was Heinke.

The return of Kaunitz to a position of influence in this sphere was probably responsible in large part for what was to become one of the best known and, from the point of view of the Church, the most insidious of Joseph's religious reforms, namely, the attack upon the monasteries.[10] The immediate cause of a policy destined to be so heavy in consequence was a modest one. A scandal had come to light in the little Carthusian monastery at Mauerbach. Some of the monks had apparently been devoting themselves to other activities than those contributing to the greater glory of God. Kaunitz brought this to the Emperor's attention and suggested that it would be well to dissolve the monastery and a number of others where similar conditions prevailed, and to use the funds which would be realized from such a dissolution to establish an Academy of Sciences, an institution which the Monarchy could well use. Once Joseph's attention had been focused upon the problem, he did not stop at such half-measures. He found that there were over 2,000 monasteries and cloisters in his domain, and something like 65,000 monks and nuns. It appeared to him that not only were these numbers inordinately large, but the vast majority of monasteries and cloisters were necessarily so small that they could have no impact whatever upon society at large. And he was soon arguing that those institutions which were of no use whatever to mankind could not be pleasing in the sight of God. The contemplative life was no longer to serve them as a *raison d'être*. If they performed no social function, they would have to go.

In January 1782 the first wave of dissolutions came. It affected the numerically less important orders, the Carthusians, Camaldulensians, and Eremites, and among the female orders, the Carmelites and Clarissians. The religious Brotherhoods and Tertiary Orders, which Joseph regarded as completely useless, were also suppressed. It is something of a paradox that among the first to be dissolved were the Eremites, who were entirely engaged in educating the children of the poor in the countryside, certainly a useful function in the Emperor's terms. But this was only a beginning. Local authorities were encouraged to submit complaints against other orders, and they were quick to follow the hint. Before long, Dominican, Benedictine, and Celestine houses were being closed. By 1786, when the dissolutions had run their course, some 738 houses had been dissolved and the number of monks and nuns had been reduced to just under 40,000.[11]

The monks belonging to the dissolved monasteries were not simply put out on the street. They had the choice of entering another house of their order, or if this was not possible for them, of going over to the secular clergy. The monks who took the latter course were to receive a pension of 200 florins yearly and those who chose to leave the country were given 100 florins as travel expenses. In spite of these fairly generous conditions, the dissolutions yielded a very sizable sum, over 32.5 million florins by 1786.[12] This huge amount exceeded by far what was needed for schemes such as the proposed Academy of Sciences. Before long, Joseph had decided to put the money which the confiscations yielded into a special religious fund which was to be used for the support of the unbeneficed secular clergy, which was frequently living at a near-starvation level. The Emperor was determined also to increase the number of secular priests, and when the Austrian hierarchy proved slow to respond to his urgings in this direction, he proceeded independently of it. On Imperial authority new parishes were to be established wherever 700 or more people lived without a church, or where worshipers had to walk for more than an hour to reach one, or where a church had been abandoned. These newly created parishes also were paid for largely out of the money taken away from the monks. It may be objected that Joseph's religious fund was a bookkeeping fiction, as in reality all moneys taken in by the Crown in his reign went into an undifferentiated central fund, but there is no doubt that all the proceeds from the confiscations and more was ultimately spent on the Church.

It was not to be expected that so important a change as the Edict of Toleration would go unchallenged by the Church authorities. In particular the Archbishop of Vienna, the ultra-conservative Hungarian magnate Cardinal Migazzi, entered a series of increasingly embittered protests.[13] When it became clear that Joseph meant to proceed with the closing of the monasteries, the Cardinal pulled all stops. It was cruel, he maintained, to force people who had voluntarily immured themselves in still tender years to go out into a world whose ways they did not know. Moreover, it was blasphemous to assert that these houses served no useful purpose. After all, whole villages, even towns, owed their preservation from disasters to the prayers which their inmates sent up to heaven. In the *Staatsrath* Kaunitz characterized this protest as senseless twaddle based on ascetic fanaticism. But Migazzi did not limit himself to complaints to the Emperor. His dispatches to Rome were filled with the most dire predictions about the fate of the whole Church if Joseph were to be allowed to go on unchecked. These were not long in having their effect.

In December 1781 the Papal Nuncio in Vienna delivered a letter to the Emperor in which His Holiness Pius VI let it be known that he wished to discuss Joseph's ecclesiastical policies "as father to son." For this purpose he proposed, in spite of his advanced years and uncertain state of health, to undertake the long journey to Vienna.[14] The immediate reaction to this startling announcement was consternation on the part of both Chancellor and Emperor. Kaunitz was afraid that Joseph, about whose personal piety he did not delude himself, would be so awed by the presence of the Pope that he would retreat from his stand. He urged Joseph to seize upon whatever excuse came to mind to prevent the visit. Joseph was not the least worried about confronting Pius, but he felt that the Pope's presence in Vienna would be the signal for all the reactionary elements in the Church to go over to the attack. Still, he did not see his way clear to putting off Pius, and the visit was duly arranged. The greatest danger from Joseph's point of view was that the Austrian bishops would avail themselves of the occasion to present personally their protests to the Pope and thus confront him with a religious cabal. Kaunitz suggested that this could easily be prevented by an Imperial order forbidding them to leave their dioceses, but Joseph felt that to deprive the Pope of the manifestation of respect due him from the dignitaries of the Church would be a gratuitous insult. His answer to the Archbishop of Prague and the Bishop of Breslau, who had inquired whether their presence in Vienna would be appropriate during the Pope's visit, was a masterpiece of innuendo: "Anyone who does not have reason to fear the law has the right to come to Vienna. All bishops are free to decide for themselves whether they wish to appear there or not."

Although he was willing to suffer the presence of Pope and bishops in his capital, Joseph did not mean to be put in the position of having to defend his measures in public. Leopold had written from Italy that it was the Pope's intention to set the tone for his visit by himself celebrating a welcome mass in St. Stephen's Cathedral and thereafter denouncing Joseph's reforms from the pulpit. Joseph informed Migazzi that if His Holiness chose to embark on such a course a scandal was unavoidable as he would then arise in the Imperial box and answer in kind. In order to prevent various unpleasantnesses from developing at the start, Joseph decided to meet the Pope in Neunkirchen. This would be a mark of his high respect for him, but also an opportunity to make it clear that he would not tolerate any appeals over his head. Pius entered Vienna with all the honors due him, but with the knowledge that any complaints would have to be addressed to Joseph and to no one else.

Pius' reception in Vienna by the populace was tumultuous, a
fact which did not escape Joseph's attention. The cortège was met
at the Hofburg by the entire Court, and Kaunitz and the rest of
the ministers were presented. According to the papal account, the
Chancellor wished to kneel before His Holiness and was only at
the last moment prevented by the Pope from doing so, although
Austrian descriptions of the scene flatly contradict this.[15] Whatever his attitude may have been in public, in private Kaunitz was
adamant about the necessity for resisting the wiles of Rome. On
the same day he submitted a memorandum to Joseph in which he
urged the Emperor to insist on his rights to carry out further monastic dissolutions, to appoint bishops in Lombardy, and to defend the Edict of Toleration. He also suggested that it would be
best if he were present during all interviews between Pope and
Emperor. But Joseph, despite the fact that he was suffering from
a stubborn eye infection which would not yield to treatment, decided to face the Pope alone. He seems to have felt that the Chancellor would prove to be an irritant and that, in his absence, a *via
media* might be agreed upon. The first interview was devoted
largely to the Emperor's exposition of the grounds which had
moved him to issue the Edict of Toleration and, according to his
own account, he was so persuasive that the Pope exclaimed at the
end that he himself could not have acted otherwise. In a second
meeting Joseph defended his suppression of the papal bulls directed against the Jansenists and again Pius seems not to have
raised serious objections. As Joseph was prevented by his illness
from participating in the traditional Easter ceremonies, Pius took
his place, to the great edification of the assembled believers.[16]

If the Pope's visit seemed to be unfolding with remarkable
smoothness, this was more appearance than reality. The really
sensitive issues—the dissolution of the monasteries and the granting of marriage dispensations—had not yet come up for discussion. In this matter Kaunitz and the Vice-Chancellor, Philip Cobenzl, were not only urging Joseph to avoid every compromise,
but demanded that he should request the Pope to submit a document stating his position so that they would be prepared to resist
any inopportune demands. After expressing some misgivings, Joseph assented to this, and a papal memorandum was duly placed
in his hands. This statement, which made it clear that there
would be no essential reconciliation between the two points of
view, contained among others the following points: The Emperor
was to take immediate measures to halt the alarming flow of de-
sertions from the Church; religious books must continue to be

censored by the Church; marriage dispensations were an ancient papal prerogative and would not be abandoned; the property of the suppressed orders was not to be taken over by the government, and new houses were to be created for those monks who had been forced to leave their old ones. Joseph's answer to all this was a masterpiece of restraint. He defended the actions he had taken, but he at the same time declared himself ready to discuss further this or that point. Thereupon Pius replied that he did not see how, if the Emperor continued to persist in these views, he could continue to consider himself a son of the Church. Joseph's rejoinder to this was not, as the papal journal asserts blandly, deep consternation at having caused the Holy Father displeasure, but rather the unequivocal observation that the secret of eating and drinking well in spite of excommunication had already been found.[17]

Since it appeared that nothing more could be accomplished, the Pope let it be known that he intended to terminate his visit. Joseph, however, was unwilling to let it go at that and begged him to stay, announcing that concessions on his part were by no means impossible. Pius, believing wrongly that only Kaunitz stood in the way of an accommodation, decided to pay the Chancellor a visit.[18] Kaunitz received him in his villa in Mariahilf, and although the account of the Chancellor's discourteous manner circulated by the Dutch Ambassador, the Protestant Count Wassenaer, is largely fictitious, nothing of substance was said. Finally, in order to put a good face on it, Joseph made some insignificant concessions, and the Pope left Vienna without an open break. Back in Italy, Pius, with a deplorable disregard for the literal truth, let it be known that Joseph had made sweeping promises to change his views on marriage dispensations, the position of the bishops, and toleration. But the Roman wits who asserted that the mass Pius had celebrated in St. Stephen's had lacked not only the *credo* for the Emperor but also the *gloria* for the Pope, knew better. The papal visit, if not precisely a fiasco, had borne no visible fruit.

Relations between Vienna and Rome did not improve in the period immediately following. In 1783 when the Archbishop of Milan died, Joseph made use of the right he had claimed in Vienna and nominated Filippo Visconti in his place. The Pope protested immediately, maintaining that this was not the Emperor's privilege and that only a papal indulgence which he had neglected to apply for, might justify this act. Kaunitz was of the opinion that the papal protest should not be dignified with an answer,

but Joseph overruled him. He wrote Pius that he had known perfectly well what he was doing when he appointed Visconti and
closed with the insistent request, just barely not an overt threat,
that His Holiness refrain from pushing things to the last extremi-
ties. But when it appeared that a break was really unavoidable, it
was nevertheless Joseph who took the initiative to avert it. The
Emperor now decided to go to Rome, in strict incognito, to negotiate with Pius. That Joseph's incognito was not as impenetrable
as he fancied, is shown by a ludicrous scene which took place
when he crossed into the Papal States. "Count Falkenstein" was
met by a host of officials and accorded royal honors. It turned out
that he had been mistaken for the King of Sweden whose visit was
expected at the same time.[19]

Although it was Joseph's intention to go to Rome, not to Ca-
nossa, he showed himself conciliatory in the Pope's presence.
After some preliminary skirmishing he accepted the papal contention that indulgences would have to be secured for all episco-
pal appointments in Lombardy. As Pius had chosen to take his
stand on this point, his victory here made it easier for him to give
way on others. Joseph's concession in the question of the bishops
was incorporated in a Concordate, published in January 1784,
and the Pope made a tacit agreement not to protest too violently
about the various other aspects of Joseph's religious policy which
displeased him. Kaunitz' judgment was that Pius had escaped
with a black eye. Perhaps the humiliation which the Pope had
been forced to endure prepared him to accept the much graver
ones which he would some years later have to accept at the hands
of Napoleon. As for Joseph's policies, while they left the Catholic
Church in a position from which it could recapture the greater
part of its lost hegemony after his death, they at least succeeded
in making a breach in what had been one of the most strongly
held ecclesiastical fortresses in Europe. The Emperor's fault was
that he did not go farther, that he refrained from disestablishing
the Church; such a step would have been the only means of assur-
ing the permanent triumph of his reforms. But disestablishment
had never been his objective.

CHAPTER X

Agricultural, Economic and Cultural Reforms

IF JOSEPH WAS, BY HIS OWN ADMISSION, AN ATHEIST IN MATTERS OF economics, his unbelief was strongly laced with elements of physiocratic theory. His concern for agriculture had already found expression in a number of measures during the co-regency, and now he proposed to bring about a long overdue recasting of the entire agricultural complex. Even if he had not been moved by considerations of humanity, the most cursory observation would have sufficed to convince him that the place to begin was at the bottom. In spite of his previous efforts the condition of the ordinary peasant was still such that it precluded even halfway efficient production. This state was due primarily to the onerous *robot,* or forced labor obligations, which, although they had been, as has been seen, somewhat reduced still took up an undue amount of the peasants' time and energies. But to abolish the *robot* would entail a basic dislocation of the Austrian economy, as the greater part of the wealth of the landed aristocracy, which in turn constituted a large segment of the national wealth, was based upon the forced labor which it had come to consider its due. To do away with the *robot* without compensation would bring about the financial ruin of the nobility and this in turn might well shake the State to its foundations. To compensate the landholders with State funds would put an intolerable strain on the budget. Joseph decided to begin with the far less complicated task of abolishing formal serfdom, that is, *Leibeigenschaft.* This was done in a decree of November 1781.

What this decree did was to make an end of the peasant's inferiority under the law. He was no longer subject to the lord's jurisdiction and was guaranteed the same civil rights that any other subject enjoyed, foremost among them the right to leave his land if he wished. This decree was meant to bring the peasantry of Bohemia, Moravia, and Silesia up to the same minimum level of freedom which Joseph assumed, as it turned out somewhat naively, already existed in his other provinces.[1] It soon became evident that this was not the case. The Estates of province after province objected and pointed out that although serfdom did not in fact exist in the regions they represented, a series of restrictions on the peasants was in force, which really amounted to the same thing and which could not be done away with without fatal damage to the economy. The Emperor was not to be put off by such arguments. If conditions tantamount to serfdom existed, these too would have to be eliminated. He appealed to the utilitarian instincts of the landowners: "Agriculture and industry can only flourish under decent freedom." Even so, in some districts, concessions had to be made. In Carniola, for instance, a peasant who wanted to leave his land had first to find an acceptable substitute and to pay the landowner a fee amounting to five percent of his property. As it happened, the dire predictions of the Estates about whole districts being emptied of peasants did not materialize.

The nobility was adversely affected in another sensitive but by no means critical area: domestic servants, underpaid and ill used, deserted their masters in droves. In numerous instances large families were left high and dry in their country residences with not so much as a slavey to tend to their needs. At last it became necessary to pass special restrictive legislation which required all domestic servants to submit notice six months in advance of quitting their positions.

The enforcement of the decree of 1781 varied greatly from province to province. In Bohemia the nobility acting in concert to exercise passive resistance essentially nullified it.[2] The Hungarian Estates proclaimed with considerable pride that the Hungarian peasant had never been a serf but was rather "a tenant in fee simple, who was fully informed as to his rights and duties by precise contracts"[3] and continued to restrict him as it had always done. In the German-speaking provinces the peasants were now somewhat better off. This was true particularly if they were involved in a legal dispute with the landowner. Henceforth, if they were unable to obtain due satisfaction in the manorial courts, they could not only appeal their cases to a royal court but were provided with legal counsel free of all costs. Also, as a sign of their emancipation, the rustics were forbidden to kiss the hand of the landowner or to bow down before him, customs which, however, proved difficult to eradicate in remote districts. In his inaugural lecture at the University of Vienna for the year 1782 Sonnenfels, exulting over what had already been accomplished, listed as the proudest achievement of a reforming Emperor the circumstance that all his subjects were now citizens.⁴ The Emperor himself knew better.

It was clear to Joseph that so long as the peasant was not freed from the burden of the *robot,* his emancipation would remain largely illusory. He might change his place of employment but would most likely encounter conditions as hard as those he had left, or perhaps worse. It was the peasantry's economic depression that was at the root of the problem and to it the Emperor devoted a major portion of his attention throughout the rest of his reign. Both Sonnenfels and his colleague Von Justi had maintained for some time that the solution of the problem was to be found in broadening the basis of landownership. Once a substantial portion of the peasantry was in hereditary possession of its land, it would be possible for every peasant, by hard work and self-discipline, to become a landowner and the peasantry would then have its proper place in society. Unfortunately, the problem was not quite so simple. It was an obvious fact that most peasants simply did not have anything like the means to buy sufficient land to make up a viable farm, and that even if funds could be found to lend them the money they would be forced to mortgage themselves so heavily that their new bondage would be worse than their old; thus, the question of the *robot* remained as vexatious as ever.

In 1783 Joseph undertook the first serious attempt to come to grips with this. In February of that year a decree was issued which laid down the bases for the commutation of the *robot* into graduated cash payments. Those peasants who owed thirteen days of forced labor annually could pay instead one gulden 30 kreutzer. The cottagers who owed twice that labor would have to pay five gulden. Additional payments were foreseen for those peasants who were obligated to bring their teams.⁵ The solution was a halfway equitable one, as the stipulated payments were within reach of at least the more prosperous peasants and represented, if not a full, at least a reasonable equivalent of their labor. Unfortunately, the vast majority of the noble proprietors, lacking that enterprising spirit which might have found new income-producing activities to invest this cash in, much preferred to retain the old forced labor. There was evidently no point in using the money to hire agricultural labor, as it would not have paid for an equivalent amount of work, and the landowners who would put their money in industrial enterprises were as yet a rarity. It is quite true that in Bohemia there were numerous examples of aristocrats investing in industrial ventures on their estates. As, however, they for the most part could not sell their lands as it was either so heavily mortgaged as to make a sale unprofitable, or entailed, these were seldom more than side lines. In consequence, the commutation decree was everywhere evaded. In Transylvania not only was there no question of introducing the commutation of services, but it turned out that the decree of 1781, putting an end to formal *Leibeigenschaft,* far from being carried out had not even been proclaimed to the population. The result was a peasant uprising which had to be put down by government troops, who thus found themselves in the position of having to support the local authorities who had deliberately sabotaged the Imperial commands.[6]

While he was achieving only an indifferent success with his attempts to improve the position of the peasant by legislation, Joseph at the same time proceeded along another avenue. He was to a considerable degree, as we have already observed, in sympathy with the views of the physiocrats and had been particularly impressed by the opinions he had heard expounded by Turgot during his first visit to France. Turgot maintained that basic to all real agricultural reform was a reform of the tax system. He proposed a single tax on land, based not on the income which any given property might produce, but rather on an arbitrary assessment of its value. In this manner a proprietor would either be forced to work his land efficiently so as to produce the maximum income from it, or to sell it to someone else who would. This was just the sort of direct and all-encompassing notion that appealed to Joseph. In 1785 he called into life a commission to draw up a register of all landed property in his dominions, which was to serve as a basis for a general reform of taxation. But the work of the commission was compromised from the beginning. The Emperor was unwilling to fly in the face of all tradition to the point of establishing really arbitrary values, and it was decided to fix these on the basis of a property's average income over the last decades. This decision inevitably gave rise to wholesale cheating. To begin with, every obstacle was put in the way of the commission and in spite of Joseph's proddings not a single acre had been surveyed by 1787. Thereupon, the head of the commission, Count Karl Zinzendorf, who had sympathized openly with the opposition to the work he was supposed to be directing, was dismissed and replaced by *Hofrath* von Eger.[7]

Now at last the commission proceeded with its work. Its final product was far from perfect; it has been estimated that in Bohemia alone 36 percent of all productive land was successfully kept from appearing on the register, but it did produce a general *Kadaster*.[8] It was now Joseph's intention to combine the new tax based thereupon with the final abolition or rather commutation of the *robot*. At this point he encountered determined opposition even among some of his closest collaborators in the *Hofkanzlei*. It was argued that the nobility would be irrevocably ruined and that a national disaster would ensue. The Chancellor, Count Rudolf Chotek, resigned rather than affixing his name to a document which he disapproved of with all his being. The Styrian Estates in a protest filled with pathos were so carried away that they made an unmistakable threat to the effect that if the proposed edict should become law their despair would know no bounds. But Joseph refused to give way, and the edict was promulgated in February 1789.[9]

At first glance, the terms of the new law were not Draconic. All land was to be taxed at the fixed rate of 12 2/9 percent yearly of its assessed value. In addition, the peasantry would pay up to an additional 17 7/9 percent of their income annually in commutation of their former obligations in *robot*.[10] Thus, in theory, every subject would retain 70 percent of his income, surely not an unreasonable share. The difficulty was that the assessments were so high that even taking into consideration the cheating that had taken place very few properties yielded anything like their assessed valuation. Moreover, in the absence of forced labor they would yield even less. In many cases the new tax would amount to 50 percent of the real income. As a hostile pamphleteer pointed out, if it cost him half of his income to obtain the Emperor's protection, he could be wiped out for lack of any protection at the end of two years and be no worse off. The argument was no less telling for being a sophism. The opposition was both vocal and general and would have to be placated before the new law became effective. Joseph was forced to begin by extending the *robot* for a year, with the proviso that the peasants should receive a wage for their labors. There, essentially, the question rested in 1790. It may be objected that Joseph was himself to blame for the difficulties with which his attempts to reform agriculture were beset, as his narrow physiocratic principles led him to greatly overestimate the ability of the landowners to pay taxes and still run their farms at a profit. But it must be remembered that at his accession, State, landlord, and Church took between them on the average 73 percent of the peasant's income.[11] This was a condition which was no longer tenable and the Emperor's attempt to redistribute rural income was both laudable and necessary.

In Hungary the situation was complicated by the privileged position of the landowners. This had been given tacit approval in the Treaty of Szatmár (1711) at which time the Hapsburgs, happy to have escaped the loss of a large part of Hungary which during the Rákóczi rebellion had appeared a distinct possibility, in essence confirmed nobiliary privileges *in toto* in return for political support from the aristocracy. Maria Theresia, who was always well-disposed toward the Magyars, was at first unwilling to abrogate these rights, which were already being regarded as traditional. Nevertheless, in 1767, genuinely shocked by a number of excesses which had recently come to light, she decreed the famous *Urbarium* which restored to the Hungarian peasant his freedom to change his place of employment at will and decreed that whenever contracts regulating socage ran out, they were to be renegotiated on terms more favorable to the peasant. Thereafter, while the landowners continued to enjoy their immunity from taxation, there was a limit to the exactions they could make upon their peasants. This cut to the bone, in part because many estates were run inefficiently, in part because Hungary labored under the disadvantage of being on the wrong side of an internal tariff wall (Hungarian wine in particular was all but priced out of the Austrian market) and Hungarian agricultural products had to be produced very cheaply in order to be at all competitive.

It is thus not in the least surprising that the Magyar nobility reacted violently to Joseph's proposed physiocratic tax. Many landowners were genuinely convinced that they would be ruined by it. To compound the evil, there was an acute shortage of trained surveyors in Hungary, and so this work was done either by foreigners or by artisans or even peasants recruited on the spot. The many complaints of the landowners that these people deliberately inflated their measurements and then demanded bribes to reduce them were probably not without foundation. As the work of the surveying commission was drawn out over the years it was only natural that the wildest rumors about what the final assessment would be were accepted as hard fact, and a rebellious spirit was the result.

If Joseph was a physiocrat, he was no less of a mercantilist. After all, he was not bound by the pedantic distinctions of the academicians and saw nothing mutually exclusive in the two systems. His duty, as he saw it, was to bring about the maximum economic development in his dominions, and this, he thought like most of his royal colleagues, could be accomplished only at the expense of other nations. Mercantilism was by no means an innovation in Austria. Under Maria Theresia it had been reinforced by political conditions, the Seven Years' War having had as an aftermath a veritable tariff war against Prussia and Saxony. As a result of this, Bohemia had been effectively barred from exporting its goods on the Elbe and the Oder and now had to ship them south. Trieste replaced Hamburg as the principal outlet of the Monarchy; costs went up as a result, but this was accepted without question in what was regarded as the national interest. When some Viennese merchants did venture to object, Joseph's answer was, "Why, it is I who am making merchants of you, hitherto you were only shopkeepers, the agents of foreigners." [12] It was his intention to produce within the boundaries of Austria most of what was consumed there. This necessitated a considerable expansion of Austrian industry. Francis Stephen had before Joseph's time contributed much in the way of material encouragement for the creation of new industries and the expansion of existing ones, particularly the manufacture of textile and glass in Bohemia, and Joseph continued these policies. Moreover, his mercantilism was not so rigid that he insisted on the inflexible central control of all industry. Rather, his industrial policy was laced with a portion of liberal doctrine which allowed a considerable latitude to the owners of factories. [13]

Unfortunately, among the essential conditions for the industrialization of the Monarchy, one at least was to a great extent lacking. Sufficient reserves of capital were not available. Or, more precisely, the wealthier aristocrats, who disposed over the greater share of capital, were not willing to invest in industry. Of the old and established families, only the Harrachs and the Kinskys had taken the plunge. And so prestigious was landownership that when an occasional merchant or banker prospered sufficiently to merit ennoblement, he more often than not hastened to convert his wealth into land, although it generally brought him considerably less. Joseph did his best to combat these attitudes. When, for instance, he made the banker Fuchs a count in 1781, he stipulated that he and his sons should remain in commerce. [14] But overcoming ancient prejudices was slow work. In order to further the development of industry, the Emperor circumscribed the considerable privileges of the craft guilds and eventually, in 1786, abolished them altogether. This undoubtedly resulted in an increase in production, but did not endear him to the artisans, who had established for themselves an enviable eminence.

The eighteenth century was par excellence the period of the immense government supported trading company, and Joseph did not mean to let the opportunity to turn a huge profit pass him by. To be sure, the most desirable market had long ago been exploited by others, but the world was large and something might yet be left for the Austrians. An Austrian East India Company was duly chartered and an expedition to the Nicobar Islands was mounted. This was not a happy choice, as these islands were wholly barren and produced nothing of value, and when a second ship found that the garrison left behind by the first had vanished without leaving a trace, the project was abandoned. Joseph's attempts to make something of the moribund Ostend Company failed because of his inability to reopen the port of Antwerp. On the whole, while the Emperor undoubtedly meant to bring about a considerable diminution of the extent to which the Monarchy depended on agriculture, and this in spite of his physiocratic convictions, his achievements were modest. This was due in part to the often haphazard and incomplete character of his economic legislation and in larger part to the impossibility of achieving basic economic transformations, at least in the short run, by ultimately political measures. That it was entirely possible to accomplish something for the long run was shown by Joseph's policy of settling the most underpopulated and backward regions of the Monarchy with peasants from the impoverished areas of southern Germany. Using methods very similar to those which the recruiters for American industry would resort to a century later, Joseph's agents traveled through these regions making extravagant promises. To the landless Swabian or Hessian, who formerly had been forced to fend off starvation by selling himself into virtual slavery as a foreign mercenary, the prospect of cheap land and favored treatment by the government was irresistible. Almost 50,000 South German peasants responded and most were settled in recently acquired Galicia but to some extent also in Transylvania.[15] The transition was often a painful one, there had been insufficient preparations made to receive the settlers, and the sum of 4,000,000 florins in subsidies which the enterprise cost could not be quickly recovered. But eventually the result was the transformation of Austrian Poland into the comparatively flourishing province which it was before the First World War, and a considerable boost to the economy of Hungary. That these settlements of German peasants would retain their national identities and stubbornly refuse to be absorbed by independent Poland and Hungary more than a century and a half later, thus becoming pliable instruments of Great German chauvinism, was of course not to be foreseen in the eighteenth century.

Unlike many great rulers who have vast resources at their disposal, Joseph was not a builder. He regarded the erection of costly new public buildings in the place of perfectly serviceable old ones as an inexcusable waste of money. He did not feel that his prestige required the erection of useless ornaments. Such buildings as he did put up were without exception functional in nature. His most ambitious project was the construction of a new General Hospital, which replaced the small and quite inadequate structure that had been put up in the middle of the previous century under Ferdinand III. In Joseph's time the *Allgemeines Krankenhaus* was, both with respect to its size and to the services it was able to provide, a genuine world wonder. Whether, on the other hand, it was so far ahead of its time as to justify its retention as the chief medical facility of Vienna almost two centuries later is open to question. As for Joseph's taste in architecture, it was no better and no worse than the average in an age which thought nothing of building a rococo façade onto a Romanesque church.

Joseph as a patron of the arts is a somewhat equivocal figure, too. He was, in spite of a somewhat blunted esthetic sense, genuinely interested in the theater. He regarded it primarily as a didactic instrument, and while such notions may be incompatible with the development of the highest form of dramatic expression, pure theater, in eighteenth-century Austria they were quite useful. Before Joseph, the theater goer in Vienna could choose only between attending the performances of fourth-rate itinerant Italian companies and a local version of the *commedia dell' arte*, cabaretistic in content, concerning itself with highly actual questions, but exceedingly vulgar and parochial. Joseph wanted a stage which would present weighty and elevated subjects for the edification of a serious audience, and which would do this in German. His proddings succeeded in calling into life a highly respectable but a little pompous court theater, which later as the *Burgtheater* would for a long time occupy pride of place among German stages. Music was less to the Emperor's taste. He had been at his parents' insistence taught to play the violin, and as a child he had been made to play in quartets with his brothers and sisters, but this did not in the end make him musical. He did think it a pity that this art was still to a large degree dominated by Italian composers and performers; he thought so not out of any feelings which we would describe as nationalistic, but rather out of the quasi-mercantilistic conviction that Austrian music should be produced in Austria. For this reason he subsidized Mozart, although the pension of 800 florins annually which he accorded him was less than modest. He did like Mozart's music, even if his comment on hearing the *Abduction from the Seraglio* ("too many notes") does not testify to a very high critical acumen. For this at least he received a fitting answer from the composer: "Exactly as many as necessary, Your Majesty." [16]

As is the case with practically all reformers, Joseph had in him a touch of the puritan. He forbade not only vulgarity on the stage but tried to legislate against such comparatively harmless diversions as the serenading of young ladies by their swains. It was his intention to rid Vienna of the swarms of prostitutes which, then as now, graced its streets after dark. At his order the *belles de la nuit* were rounded up, had their hair cut short and were put back on the streets, but in the daytime and with brooms in their hands. As this was unseemly and gave rise to many ludicrous scenes, it was suggested to him that it might be more realistic to gather the ladies in licensed and supervised houses. The Emperor's comment on this proposal showed that he was not unaware of certain grotesque aspects of the situation. "Much cheaper," he said, "to put a roof over the whole of Vienna." But the measure which proved completely unenforceable was his decree that the dead were hereafter to be buried not in coffins but in burlap sacks. This, he pointed out, would result in a considerable saving. His subjects, however, were not to be convinced. The outcry was so strident that the decree had to be quickly repealed.

There is no question but that many of the Emperor's failures are to be traced to his own shortcomings. His brother Leopold, in a journal which he kept in a secret script of his own devising, characterized him as ambitious but harsh; wanting to get everything done at once but being himself too lazy to go into a question thoroughly; despotic and unwilling to suffer the least contradiction; tending to surround himself with sycophants and always going by his first impression of people; obsessed by military affairs for which he had no talent whatever; always striving for effect and desperately concerned with what the mass thought of him; always favoring general panaceas over more modest but practical notions; spending the greater part of his time giving audiences to the dregs of the population, and succeeding in being feared by all but loved by none.[17] While it is surely no compliment to Joseph that the brother in whom he confided more than in any other human being should secretly have entertained such notions of him, this appraisal should not be taken at face value. Leopold had probably never forgiven Joseph for his parsimony in distributing their father's inheritance and moreover entertained equally venomous opinions about the other members of their large but divided family. *Bruderzwist im Hause Hapsburg* (sibling rivalry among the Hapsburgs) was, after all, nothing new. Still, we can grant him the accuracy of a number of his observations, even if they are put rather too strongly. Joseph was anything but tactful and could offend more people in a shorter time than any of his contemporaries. The fact that his patience was often tried beyond its not very extended limits by having to deal with a society in which obscurantism, immobilism, and plain inefficiency had acquired the stature of traditional virtues, may serve him as a partial excuse. Nevertheless, there is no question that he might have avoided much in the way of unpleasantness by the exercise of better judgment of people and a modicum of tact. But there can be no question of ascribing the essential and ultimate failure of his work to such peccadillos. His three greatest concerns, the reform of administration, Church, and rural society, were massive problems, the attempt to cope with which successfully might well have required direct or even brutal methods. And even considering that Joseph was not to have sufficient time at his disposal to do this, his work might not have been as ephemeral as it turned out to be, had he not compromised it with repeated and drearily unsuccessful ventures in the military and foreign fields. It is to these we must now turn.

CHAPTER XI

In the End—Failure

JUST BEFORE MARIA THERESIA DIED JOSEPH HAD, IN THE COURSE OF his visit to Russia, given a new and, he thought, definitive direction to the foreign policy of Austria. The debacle of the "Potato War" had convinced him at last of the jejune nature of the Kaunitzian system. The support of France was not to be counted on, if the Monarchy were to achieve any of its aims; a new and more reliable confederate would have to be found, and Russia appeared to be naturally suited for this role. The Empire of the Czars was well on the way to settling its longstanding account with the Turks, but the job was not finished, and to finish it the Russians would require, at the very least, the benevolent neutrality of Austria. In return for his support of Catherine's designs on the Ottoman Empire, Joseph could reasonably expect Russian support for his various designs in Western Europe and Russian acquiescence in enterprises of his own in the Balkans. In 1782 the heir to the Russian throne, Crown Prince Paul, visited Vienna. The personality of this young man was not such as to inspire much confidence in his host. The Czarevitch was moody, almost pathologically suspicious and filled with a mystical longing for the return of the old order in Russia. Moreover, he had never made a secret of his intense admiration for Frederick the Great. Joseph went to considerable trouble to charm his difficult guest, sparing no expense to entertain him, and then passed him on to Leopold in Florence. To the latter Paul made it clear that he disapproved of his mother's policy in its entirety and that he proposed to flog, break on the wheel, or exile all her ministers once he came to the throne.[1] It thus became self-evident that any advantages to be gotten from a Russian alliance would have to be extracted in Catherine's lifetime.

In view of this the more reasonable policy might have been to write off the bond with Russia as too tenuous to be genuinely useful and to cast about for another general guideline, but the Emperor decided in favor of the short term. In the fall of 1782 Catherine submitted to Joseph a vast and ambitious plan. She proposed that the two of them take advantage of the great struggle which France and England were waging against each other, by proceeding against the Turks. Prussia, isolated for the moment, would be unable to oppose them. It would be possible, by resorting merely to threats, to establish a Christian principality in Rumania (which, she did not take the trouble to add, would of course be a Russian client state) and to acquire some districts on the Black Sea for Russia; Austria could at the same time acquire the northern part of Serbia. If, contrary to her expectation, the Turks would not yield to pressure, Austria and Russia would crush them together. She would reestablish the Byzantine Empire for her grandson Constantine, and Joseph could have the western Balkans.[2] Both Joseph and Kaunitz were agreed that the second plan was visionary to the point of insanity, but they thought that the first one was quite capable of realization. The Austrians now joined the Russians in exerting diplomatic pressures on the Turks. Unfortunately, before any decisive results could be achieved, England and France concluded peace and it was now to be feared that further steps might lead to a general war, as the Turks had reacted to this latest development by becoming suddenly intransigent. Kaunitz, rather uncharacteristically, was at this point in favor of assuming the risk of a great European conflict, but Joseph, also playing an unaccustomed part, held back. The final result was that the Russians made off with some not inconsiderable frontier districts in the Black Sea region and the Austrians emerged empty-handed.

Again, this result should have demonstrated to Joseph the imperfect nature of his political premises, but he chose to ignore the lesson. If the East was momentarily closed to him, he still had plans in the West, and these he proposed to realize with the help of Russia. Something that had galled him ever since his visit to the Netherlands had been the attenuated nature of the economic prosperity of this region, due to the blockade by the Dutch of the Scheldt and its great port, Antwerp. He now judged that the time had come to eliminate this regrettable condition along with the so-called barrier fortresses which the Dutch had maintained in Belgium ever since the Peace of Westphalia. So far as these last were concerned, the Austrians achieved a rapid success. In fact, the fortresses were not any longer seriously held, in several the garrisons had sunk to ten men or less, and the Dutch did not propose to try to hold on to a hopeless and ridiculous position. They informed the Austrians that they were prepared to negotiate an evacuation of the fortress. Emboldened by this easy victory, Joseph decided to tackle the much more complex matter of the Scheldt. In October 1784 he ordered a brigantine, the *Louis* to proceed down-river from Antwerp. A Dutch squadron was at anchor near the river mouth and, at the appearance of the Austrian ship, challenged it. When the Austrian failed to heed this signal he was fired upon and thereupon beat a retreat. There had now been an incident which could be interpreted as an insult to the Imperial flag, and Joseph was determined to make an issue of it. The Dutch were threatened with war and Austrian troops were concentrated near the frontier. At the critical moment it turned out, however, that a) Russia was in no position whatever to give the Austrians any help; b) the French might very well support Holland; c) the Austrian army was not ready for war; and d) the campaigning season was over anyway. Reluctantly, Joseph had to content himself with the making of threats. After complicated negotiations in 1785 the Dutch were finally moved to the payment of an indemnity for the incident of the *Louis,* but the Scheldt remained just as effectively closed. It was a poor harvest.[3]

If the Russians had done nothing for Austria in the dispute with Holland, they at least made some effort to support Joseph in an enterprise which was even closer to his heart and which he launched at about the same time. He had never really reconciled himself to the unfavorable issue of the "Potato War." Although at the time he had himself, by giving way to near-panic, contributed to the abandonment of the venture, he soon afterward convinced himself that he had been robbed of success by a loss of nerve on the part of Maria Theresia. The fascination of Bavaria had not worn off for him, and as that province continued to be misgoverned under Karl Theodor, it appeared to the Emperor that the question might be reopened with profit. The Elector still had no legitimate male issue, he had not overcome his dislike for Munich, and the Austrian representative at his court, Baron Lehrbach, reported that he was only too willing to listen to reasonable proposals. Joseph now settled on a scheme which had already been considered in 1778, only to be discarded again, namely, an exchange of the Netherlands for Bavaria. The Austrian Netherlands, although undoubtedly one of the most economically developed provinces of the Monarchy, were not contiguous with it. As they were far away, and as the population clung tenaciously to its ancient and traditional rights, which had been successfully maintained against Spaniards as well as Austrians, they were not only difficult to govern but did not fit well into the

Emperor's plans to centralize the administration of his domains. They were, moreover, indefensible in a serious conflict, and thus their maintenance stipulated an eventual dependence upon the good-will of France. It might well be worth the game if all of Bavaria could be acquired in return.

Joseph and Kaunitz worked out a plan which appeared to be eminently promising. Karl Theodor was to be offered the Netherlands along with some minor possessions of Austria in the West, and the whole was to be elevated into a Kingdom of Burgundy. The transfer was to be made palatable to the French by giving them Luxemburg. The Emperor remembered only too painfully that Frederick of Prussia had not hesitated to go to war on the occasion of his previous attempt to swallow Bavaria, but the picture, he reckoned, had now entirely changed. The King would never dare to challenge an Austria supported by both France and Russia, and, furthermore, he was not gaining in strength. It would be a straightforward exchange, one province for another. The Prussians would have no reason to feel threatened. Joseph also recalled that Karl Theodor's legal heir, Duke Karl August of Zweibrücken, had been one of the chief roadblocks to the Austrian designs seven years earlier. This obstacle was now to be removed with the help of Russia.

It was well known in Vienna that Karl August was able to maintain himself in princely style in the miniscule state of Zweibrücken only with the help of a considerable French subsidy. But at the conclusion of their war against England the French were at the point of national bankruptcy and were trying to cut corners wherever possible. There was good reason to suppose that Karl August's subsidy would be considerably reduced or even cut off entirely. It was also known that he had lately formed a friendship with the Russian representative in nearby Frankfort, Count Romantsov. The Austrians now prevailed upon the Russian Court to instruct Romantsov to win over the Duke to the exchange project. He was to promise him that Austria would take up the slack if his source of French income were to dry up and to whet his appetite for the royal crown which, in the normal course of events, he would wear one day. At first all went well. Karl August seemed at least interested enough to consider the proposition. At this point, however, Joseph spoilt the game by falling back upon greengrocer's accounts. He had convinced himself, on the basis of questionable records, that the total annual income of Bavaria was a million or so below that of the Netherlands. As he did not wish to accept such a reduction of income, he now proposed to retain

Luxemburg to make up the difference. This of course did away with the all-important *douceur* to the French, who at once not only lost all interest, but now bethought themselves that the exchange, which would replace a vulnerable province on their borders with an independent realm that might one day prove troublesome, was not at all in their national interest. They thereupon gave Karl August an assurance that his subsidy would continue undiminished, and they saw to it that information about the plan was leaked to Prussia. Frederick did not hesitate to take appropriate steps. He organized a league of German principalities, the *Fürstenbund*, to safeguard the territorial integrity of the Empire, and let it be known that if necessary he would again take up the sword. Catherine informed Joseph that in view of the changed circumstances she could no longer support him. The exchange had to be dropped, this time for good, and with it the chance of creating an effective barrier to the eventual domination of Germany by Prussia. When rumors of what had been afoot began to circulate rather freely, Joseph's popularity in Belgium, which after all he had prepared to give away without so much as a by-your-leave from the inhabitants, was not enhanced. Still, the fiasco might have brought with it at least one benefit. It should now have been abundantly clear that the support of Russia in major diplomatic ventures was not to be counted on or was at least insufficient. But Joseph refused to draw the obvious conclusion. Or, more precisely, it was Kaunitz who insisted on the retention of this unpromising line of policy. When Frederick the Great died in August 1786 Joseph thought that the opportunity might be at hand for a rapprochement with Prussia, which might have ushered in a basic reorientation of Austrian policy. But the Chancellor would not hear of it and insisted that the Monarchy's only salvation lay in close cooperation with Russia.

Toward the end of 1786 Joseph received an invitation from the Empress Catherine to join her on a tour of inspection of her recently acquired territories in the Crimea. Joseph thought the invitation lacked somewhat in formality and in the respect due him. In addition he was anything but well. He had aged considerably since 1780. He had lost all his hair, his complexion was sallow, he walked with a now habitual stoop, he was always tired. The Prussian ambassador intimated maliciously that these symptoms were due to a syphilitic infection the Emperor had contracted during casual amusements. But in spite of the state of his health and of his wounded pride, Joseph considered the opportunity to come to an agreement with Catherine about the aggrandizement of their respective realms too good to miss. The Prince de Ligne was sent to Russia to prepare the way and by the middle of April 1787 Joseph had followed him.[4] After their meeting the two sovereigns traveled south in state, accompanied by the whole diplomatic corps. It was Catherine's intention to impress Joseph with the strength and resources at her disposal, and he was careful to utter nothing but praise for what he saw. In reality he looked upon Prince Potemkin's efforts as an enormous waste of manpower and money and thought that although the area was evidently a rich one, the Russians would never accomplish anything without more rational methods.

Be that as it may, the real purpose of his visit as he saw it was to elicit an agreement from Catherine to join him in a campaign against the Turks. The Empress was not slow in making overtures to him. Was he not, she asked, consumed with the desire to recover what had been taken from his ancestors, to recapture Belgrade? Joseph answered that while he did not consider himself lacking in zeal when it came to asserting his rights over what was rightfully his, he was forced to take into consideration the positions of France and Prussia. Catherine dismissed these reservations by pointing out that Prussia without Frederick was not to be taken seriously and that France was hard put to keep from breaking up over its financial difficulties and should not be considered a threat. She herself was strong enough to defeat the Turks alone so long as Austria did not oppose itself to her designs. The opportunity was really too good to be missed.[5] Joseph thought this appraisal of the situation rather too roseate and told Potemkin that if the French were to agree to what would amount to a partition of the Ottoman Empire, they would, at the very least, have to be promised Egypt and Crete. To this last the Russians objected as they themselves wanted that island. These vast plans must have had something of an intoxicating effect on Joseph, but he retained enough detachment to agree, for the moment at least, to no more than Austrian support for a Russian *démarche* at Constantinople, in which the Turks were to be called upon for the very last time to put an end to their harassment of the Balkan Christians and their raids upon Russian commerce. If, as was to be expected for no other reason than the lack of control which the Porte exercised over its Beys, the Turks did not comply, the Austrians and the Russians would consult again.[6]

While Joseph was still engaged upon these negotiations, he received the most unwelcome news that a revolt had broken out in the Austrian Netherlands, and he was forced to leave Russia before having reached a definite and detailed agreement with Catherine. The Belgian troubles were, at least indirectly, the result of the miscarried Bavarian venture.⁷ Having had to reconcile himself to keeping Belgium after all, Joseph had, by his lights, made the best of the situation and decided upon the introduction of his various centralizing measures into this province, which had so far been largely exempt from them. The Belgians, next door to Calvinist Holland, had developed a certain rigidity in their Catholicism, which in the absence of political independence had come to incorporate for them quasi-national values, and they bitterly resented the anti-clerical portion of the Josephinian system. The trouble began, of all places, among seminarians. Joseph had ordered the closing of the seminaries and their students had been put in State schools which were meant to prepare them for the clergy away from the nefarious influence of the bishops. There were soon complaints that the food in these institutions was miserable and the seminarians demonstrated in the streets of several principal towns. These demonstrations were taken advantage of by wider segments of the population for the purpose of expressing their dissatisfaction with the ecclesiastical policy of the government. Worse, the Estates of Brabant, controlled by progressive and fairly liberal-minded merchants, did not hesitate to make common cause with the clerical reactionaries, and taking their stand on the ancient privilege granted them, the *Joyeuse Entrée,* refused to vote the taxes that were due.

The apparent paradox of these people supporting what were, after all, the spokesmen of an undisguised clerical obscurantism is explained by the rather peculiar political and social conditions that obtained in Belgium. The Austrian regime, while it had made no serious attempts to interfere with the traditional political liberties of the provinces, had also acquiesced in the continuing closure of the port of Antwerp. As a result the commercial prosperity that had characterized Belgium in the late Middle Ages was no more than a dim memory and there had been a considerable reversion to agriculture. As the Church owned something like half of the arable land, its influence on the economy was considerable. Such commercial ventures as had survived were hemmed in by rigid guild regulations, in effect restricting membership in these organizations to close relatives of members and preventing very effectively any projects for large-scale economic expansion. In these circumstances the merchant class was notably free of the entrepreneurial spirit that elsewhere was a mark of the times. Its profits were modest, but they could be depended upon, and so any attack upon the status quo had come to be regarded as dangerous to a condition that suited all men of property. When, in the course of the revolution which followed, genuinely radical and democratic elements, whose existence had been unsuspected, came to the fore, both the clerical dissidents and a majority of the liberal-minded merchants were to rally to the Austrian authorities with an almost unseemly haste.

Soon mobs were demanding the recall of the Emperor's representative, Count Belgioioso. The Governors, Joseph's sister Maria Christina and her husband, Albert, lost their nerve and granted all the demands made of them. There was a triumphal parade in Brussels, with music, cockades in the national colors, and slogan-bearing placards, and their highnesses themselves participated in the procession, drawn in a coach from which the populace had unhitched the horses. When Joseph heard what had taken place, he could barely control his rage. He recalled that unhappy couple to Vienna, but for the moment he did not have the means to recall the rebels to order. In consequence, he had to suffer the presence of a Belgian delegation in the Hofburg and to listen to the revindications it presented with an appearance of good grace. He was, however, only biding his time. As he insisted to his intimates, he would make an example of those who had dared to flout his authority. When sufficient Austrian troops had been assembled in the Netherlands, he withdrew the concessions that had been made by his sister. This led to a renewal of the riots and when the general in command in Belgium did not dare to order his soldiers to open fire upon the demonstrators, Joseph replaced him with one who did. The rebellion was suppressed, but what followed upon it was no more than an uneasy truce.

During these Belgian complications the situation in the East had not remained static. Perhaps the Turks believed that Austria was still neutralized by her enmity for Prussia; perhaps also the Sultan, Abdul Hamid, had resolved the diplomatic equation differently than Catherine. Whatever the reason, the Turks decided in August 1787 that the moment had arrived to recover the ground recently lost to Russia.[8] The Russian ambassador was summoned before the throne and asked to give assurances that his country's aggressive measures against Turkish shipping in the Black Sea would be stopped at once. When he protested that his instructions did not enable him to give such assurances, he was unceremoniously carted off to the notorious prison of the Seven Towers. Without awaiting the Russian reaction to this outrage, the Turks declared war. If Catherine and Potemkin's appraisal of the situation had been at all accurate, the Turks themselves had now provided them with the opportunity which they had not quite dared to create. Joseph did not hesitate to assure his ally that he intended to carry out to the full his part of the bargain.

If, however, the Austrians had fancied that their part of the operations would consist of gathering in border provinces in the northern Balkans while the Turks were crushed by the great might of the Muscovite army, they were to be bitterly disappointed. The Prince de Ligne, who had been left behind at the headquarters of Potemkin, now improbably functioning as Russian commander in chief, submitted a plan on behalf of Joseph which assumed that the main Russian effort would be directed against the Turkish position to the north of the mouth of the Danube and promised an Austrian offensive against the defenses of Belgrade. The Russians professed to be bitterly disappointed with this plan and demanded an Austrian offensive south of the Dniester into Moldavia.[9] The Russians finally accepted the Austrian plan but with much grumbling, which did not augur well for future cooperation between the allies.

It must be said to Joseph's credit that he did not enter this conflict with any inflated expectations. He had not been seduced by Potemkin's immoderate and grandiloquent speeches, he had no serious hopes of conquering a significant part of the Ottoman Empire. At best, he thought that the Austrian position on the shores of the Adriatic might be strengthened somewhat. Instead of expecting to achieve great things in this war, he regarded it as something of a necessary evil which would, however, strengthen the alliance with Russia, and thus his own position vis-à-vis Prussia. It is difficult to conceive of a more naive, not to say fatuous, series of premises and they were not long in garnering a just reward. The Prussians succeeded almost at once in persuading the Swedes to attack Russia. Catherine's forces were thus tied up in the north and were in no position to deliver a telling blow against the Ottomans. Instead of gathering effortlessly the fruits of a crushing Russian victory, Joseph had to face the main body of the Turkish army. Even so, his prospects of victory appeared bright on paper. The Turks, as usual, had decided on war before doing anything to prepare for it, and some months were to pass before their forces were in condition to fight. The Austrians had at their disposal over 200,000 men who were excellently equipped and possessed a massive preponderance in artillery. But the plans for the operation had been drawn up by Field Marshal Lacy who now demonstrated that it was by no means impossible to improve on the inanities which he had perpetrated in the "Potato War." The Austrian army began its attack on a front of some 200 miles, much too wide for it to achieve a decisive breakthrough. To this mistaken strategic concept was added the handicap of the indifferent and indolent generalship which had been the curse of Austrian arms since the beginning of the century. At the least sign of resistance, the Austrian armies halted their advance and settled down to see what the enemy would do. And Joseph's decision to assume the supreme command merely compounded the evil. His abilities as a leader of troops were at best modest, his health had been uncertain for some time, and all he achieved was that the blame for the fiasco which was rapidly assuming alarming proportions, was more firmly attached to himself.

After the Austrians had bungled to no effect for some time, the Turks launched an attack of their own against the Banat of Temesvar, and the success of this operation threatened the position of the whole Austrian army. Joseph roused himself sufficiently to transfer the full of his forces eastward to meet this new threat, but this transfer led to the most humiliating episode in the whole campaign. During a night march a false report that the Turks had been sighted led to panic and a *sauve-qui-peut,* which the enemy promptly took advantage of, and before order could be restored over 10,000 men had been lost. The Austrian army, seriously depleted by malaria and dysentery, seemed no longer able to perform the simplest maneuvers. And, equally bad, the Emperor's health had been broken completely under the strain of campaigning in these unhealthy regions. He had been subject to fits of coughing and sleeplessness when he assumed command of his armies, and before long he came down with an intermittent fever. By the end of 1788 it was evident that he was suffering from tuberculosis. Sick and discouraged, he returned to Vienna and turned over the command of the armies to Marshal Laudon. This officer was able to restore the situation and under his at least competent leadership the heavier weight of the Austrian metal was at last made to tell. The Turks were driven back, even Belgrade was captured. A juncture with the Russians, who had finally bestirred themselves in that sector, was achieved in Moldavia. But the essential damage had been done. Not only had Joseph forfeited his health, which was so essential to him if he were to be the driving force behind his by no means completed reforms, but the series of military disasters he had suffered had given heart to his opponents everywhere. Instead of strengthening his hand, the Turkish war brought on the necessity of coming to grips once more with the internal opponents of Joseph's centralism. For this he no longer had the strength.

The first fruit of Joseph's debacle in the East was insurrection. In Hungary Joseph's legislation had never been accepted in good grace. The 300,000 odd Magyar nobles, who regarded themselves as unjustly robbed of their ancient privileges, were merely biding their time. At the beginning of the Turkish war the Prussians introduced agents into the country who distributed anti-Austrian literature. By the end of 1789 there were open demands being heard for the convocation of the Hungarian Diet and it was generally understood that its first task would be to sever the Hungarian lands from the Monarchy. In the face of these threats, Joseph capitulated. The administrative reforms which had so angered the Magyars were repealed. Of all Joseph's work only the Edict of Toleration and the decree liberating the serfs were to remain in force in Hungary. Affairs in Belgium were in an even worse state. There the uneasy truce which followed upon the intervention of Austrian troops at the Emperor's orders was stretched beyond the breaking point by the lack of tact shown by the Austrian commander and by the catastrophic winter of 1788–89 which also did so much to bring about the much more portentous crisis in France. By the spring of 1789 the Austrian Netherlands were again in open revolt. Joseph, sick and discouraged, hesitated to give the order to proceed against the rebels with all the force available, and the Great Revolution in France moved him to caution as well. Before he had decided what to do, all of Belgium was in the hands of the rebels and seemed lost to Austria for all time.

It is doubtful whether Joseph realized the full implications of what was happening in Paris and Versailles. He characterized these events as incredible and confessed that he could not foresee where they would lead, but he did not hesitate to observe that Austria could benefit from the momentary inability of France to function as a great power.[10] He certainly did not realize that all of Europe was on the brink of an agonizing upheaval, but then neither did many of his most astute contemporaries. The revolution in France was for him essentially a confirmation of the increasingly cynical thesis which he had been formulating since his return from the army: there was really no point in exerting oneself for the people, they never understood what one wanted to do for them, they insisted on doing it for themselves. And then, of course, they inevitably did the wrong thing. There is even a story, perhaps worthy of credence, to the effect that the dying Emperor wanted to revoke all of his reforms and was only with difficulty dissuaded from this course.

But in Hungary, at least, immediate measures had to be taken. The ill-will that the Magyar nobles had for many years harbored against Joseph was now reinforced by a general conviction that the Emperor was no longer in effective control. In all parts of the country aristocratic landowners organized public protest meetings at which, characteristically, Latin translations of the *Marseillaise* and the *Ça ira* were sung. It seemed as if here too a backward-looking aristocratic rebellion was on the point of opening the door to a social upheaval of incalculable consequences. Kaunitz was convinced, apparently without anything in the way of tangible evidence, that Prussian agents were at work in Hungary. This last consideration, and the *exemplum horribilis* of what had taken place in Belgium, moved Joseph to issue the rescript of January 30, 1790, in which he annulled all of his reforms in Hungary, with the exception of the Edict of Toleration and the laws regulating serfdom. It was to be left to his brother and successor Leopold to follow a similar course in the rest of the Hapsburg dominions.

By the beginning of 1790 there was, at any rate, no longer any doubt possible about the fact that Joseph was dying. He himself took the blow with equanimity. He continued to work as much as his fading strength permitted him, he himself supervised the preparations for his forthcoming State funeral, and he summoned Leopold to his bedside so that he could give him his last instructions. But the wily Archduke refused to come. He had not been chary of private criticisms of his brother's measures when things started going badly, and he had no wish to be associated with him now in the popular mind. He proposed to follow a very different course when he ascended the throne, and he refused to come, remarking to his intimates that Joseph's death agonies were really taking rather too long. Kaunitz, who with his well-known horror of illness had avoided seeing the Emperor for almost three years, was of the same opinion. Joseph died on the morning of February 20, 1790, alone and regretted by few. Those of his subjects whose lives had been enhanced by his reforms were too angry about the economic conditions, which were bad as the result of the Turkish war, to recall what he had done for them.

Joseph II has been depicted, variously, as a social reformer before his time; as an apostle of German nationalism; as an embittered enemy of the aristocracy; as a dupe of anti-clerical elements; as the one force that saved Austria from the horrors of the French

Revolution; and as an inveterate bungler, whose tactlessness vitiated any chance his ambitious undertakings might have had. He was, in fact, none of these.

His reforms were without exception functional in nature, meant to assure the smoother performance of the State, which Joseph, like the majority of his royal contemporaries, had come to regard as the *summum bonum*. To be sure, this was a palpable improvement over the merely dynastic concerns of his predecessors, but it was still a far cry from the melioristic and egalitarian views which would come into their own in the following century.

While there is no doubt that Joseph wished to do away with the linguistic confusion that obtained in his scattered dominions and thought of himself eventually as a *German* ruler, he was anything but a nationalist, or even a precursor of nationalism. He founded and supported schools in diverse languages, he subsidized non-German writers. The fact that he was determined to abolish the medieval anachronism of administrative Latin in Hungary does not make him, per se, a suppressor of the Magyars. And if he thought that the primary loyalty of his peoples was to the State, rather than to their national traditions, he did not differ in this from any other autocrat.

There is, again, no lack of examples of Joseph's having turned his wrath upon individual aristocrats, nor of pronouncements of his being sharply critical of the do-nothing *noblesse*. But this was not because he wanted to abolish it as a class, nor even to systematically reduce its importance. It was merely a question of his fundamental conviction that great power entails great responsibility and that thus the aristocracy should set an example of industry and devotion to duty. The nobleman who failed in this was, in his eyes, much more culpable than the ordinary subject. What the Emperor really had in mind was the transformation of the Austrian aristocracy into a class which was, on the Prussian model, the first servant of the State after the monarch.

If Joseph did not want to extirpate the nobility, a fortiori he did not mean to crush the Catholic Church in Austria. Nor was he unaware that certain of the people he employed in the course of his ecclesiastical reforms were convinced anti-clericals. He was confident that he could make good use of them to reduce the political pretensions of the Church to what he considered was appropriate in a modern State, but he did not intend to go farther. It would not occur to anyone to characterize Richelieu or Louis XIV, who did as much in this direction and with fewer misgivings, as enemies of the Church.

Joseph manifestly did not forestall the outbreak of a revolution on the French pattern in Austria. The basis for such an upheaval was simply not present, with the exception of Belgium where a revolt did occur. The nobility, far from reaching back into a *frondeur* past and attempting to reassert half forgotten privileges, had reconciled itself since the previous century to living off the good-will, if not the bounty, of the State and was offering no effective opposition to whatever reduction in its economic position the Emperor had decided upon. The bourgeoisie was just getting a solid foothold. The artisanate, which had hedged its position in with increasingly high barriers, was to be sure faced with a large group of disaffected journeymen who could not attain masterships, but these people were neither articulate nor organized enough to be dangerous. Above all, the Monarchy was not sufficiently urbanized. Any revolt could have been nothing but a *jacquerie.* The real paradox is that had Joseph's reforms been more successful, he would have created the conditions which would have made a French Revolution possible in Austria.

It would be foolish to maintain that Joseph was not tactless or rude or uncompromising when he thought he was in the right. He was all of these things and more. It can only be said in his defense that the goals he had set for himself were ambitious and the difficulties he encountered aggravating. Few other countries could have offered such infuriating and pigheaded resistance to what was, after all, nothing more than the spirit of the times. Joseph once complained to the Prince de Ligne: "What am I to do in a country without any spirit or soul, without ambition or comprehension of what work is about?" [11] It was a harsh judgment, uttered no doubt in a despondent mood. But then, the Emperor cannot be accused of not having known his subjects.

Joseph was an autocrat in the best Western tradition. He had inherited a great power, Austria, which had lately been much abused by a formerly small one, Prussia. It was his intention to correct this unhappy situation. He was educated and intelligent enough to realize that the modernization of his dominions, which alone would make this possible, entailed a more equitable treatment of his subjects. Having set himself this task, he was fortunate to find, as a legacy from previous reigns, a reforming bureaucracy composed of men such as Kaunitz, Kressl, and Pergen, who were capable of working out the necessary program of reform. Unfortunately this was not enough. The Austrians, it turned out, were neither as industrious nor as malleable as the Prussians. Worse, the Austrian Monarchy was made up of diverse

and essentially unassimilated national units, and although the
national tensions which would ultimately tear the Monarchy
apart were for the time relatively quiescent, they could always be
and were generally used to foment sufficient trouble to vitiate the
effectiveness of Joseph's centralizing measures. And, if one accepts
the hypothesis that the Josephinian reforms were in the first instance a means to an end, Joseph, unlike Frederick William I of
Prussia, was unwilling to confine himself to building for the future. He insisted on reaping as he sowed, and as he had but little
talent for diplomacy or military affairs, his failures in these areas
merely compromised his intended program. Thus, Joseph spent
the better part of his life tilting with windmills.

His brother Leopold lived for only two years after succeeding
him on the throne, and with his death in 1792 all attempts to
continue with what was rescuable in the Josephinian program
were abandoned. As a result, when the Napoleonic tempest de-
scended upon Austria in full force, largely as retaliation for an
ill-advised and badly mismanaged attempt to crush the French
Revolution, she was ill-prepared to cope with it. Even though Joseph's reforms were hardly responsible for the occupation of Versailles by the French mob, their failure contributed heavily to the
installation of Bonaparte in Schönbrunn in 1805.

Notes and References

CHAPTER I

1. The best treatment of Austrian affairs immediately prior to Maria Theresia's accession is O. Redlich, *Das Werden einer Grossmacht: Österreich 1700–1740*. For Maria Theresia's reign the standard work remains A. von Arneth's monumental *Geschichte Maria Theresias* in ten volumes. The best biography of the Empress is E. Guglia, *Maria Theresia: Ihr Leben und ihre Regierung*, 2 vols.

2. The standard work on Joseph remains P. von Mitrofanov, *Joseph II., seine politische und Kulturelle Tätigkeit*, 2 vols. The most complete biography in English is S. K. Padover, *The Revolutionary Emperor: Joseph the Second 1741–1790*.

3. For an extended discussion of Joseph's education, see my "The Origins of Josephinism: Two Studies," in *The Colorado College Studies*, VII, 1964.

4. On Francis Stephen, H. L. Mikoletzky, *Kaiser Franz I. Stephan und der Ursprung des Hapsburgisch-Lothringischen Familienvermögens*, and F. Hennings, *Und sitzet zur linken Hand: Franz Stephan von Lothringen*.

5. This memorandum is printed in A. von Arneth, *Maria Theresia und Joseph II.: Ihre Correspondenz* (3 vols.) I, 1–12.

6. For an account of Joseph's first marriage, see F. Fejtö, *Un Habsbourg revolutionnaire: Joseph II*, pp. 47–58.

CHAPTER II

1. On Kaunitz, see G. Küntzel, *Fürst Kaunitz-Rittberg als Staatsmann*, and A. Novotny, *Staatskantzler Kaunitz als Geistige Persönlichkeit*. For the increasingly important role Kaunitz began to assume in the conduct of the internal affairs of Austria, see F. Walter, "Kaunitz' Eintritt in die innere Politik," *Mitteilungen des österreichischen Instituts für Geschichtsforschung*, XLVI.

2. Padover, *op. cit.*, p. 34.

3. Joseph to Maria Theresia, 29 May 1761, Arneth, *Maria Theresia und Joseph*, I, 12–13.

4. For a rather impressionistic but plausible discussion of Isabella's complex nature, see E. Benedikt, *Kaiser Joseph II*, pp. 23–28.

5. This tale was spread, and quite possibly invented, by the memoirist Karoline Pichler. See V. Bibl, *Kaiser Joseph II*, 37–38.

6. That Frederick was anything but elated over the necessity to acquiesce in Joseph's election is shown by his treatment of the subject in his memoirs. Here he is concerned to demonstrate that he had been perfectly able to continue the war in 1763, and says nothing about this concession. See Frederick II of Prussia, *Mémoires depuis la paix de Hubertsbourg 1763 jusqu'à la fin du partage de la Pologne 1775*, in *Oeuvres Posthumes*, V, 13–21.

7. J. W. Goethe, *Dichtung und Warheit*, Part I, Book 5.

8. Thus Bibl, *op. cit.*, 41. Cf. Joseph to Maria Theresia, April 4, 1764, Arneth, *Maria Theresia und Joseph*, I, 74–77.

9. Maria Theresia foresaw the difficulties which this approach would

encounter, but decided in favor of the attempt for the sake of Joseph. See her memorandum on the subject in Arneth, *Maria Theresia und Joseph*, I, (n.) 111–114.

10. F. Schreyvogel, *Ein Jahrhundert zu früh: Das Schicksal Josephs II.*, pp. 53–55.

11. Mikoletzky, *op. cit.*, 24–29.

CHAPTER III

1. Fejtö, *op. cit.*, 73–76.

2. Maria Theresia to Leopold, end of August 1765, in A. von Arneth, *Briefe der Kaiserin Maria Theresia an ihre Kinder und Freunde* (4 vols.) I, 21–25.

3. Benedikt, *op. cit.*, 45–48.

4. Padover, *op. cit.*, 63.

5. This memorandum is reproduced in A. von Arneth, *Maria Theresia und Joseph II*, III, 335–61.

6. A. von Arneth, *Geschichte Maria Theresia* (10 vols.) VII, 199.

7. Thus Padover, *op. cit.*, 65.

8. Fejtö, *op. cit.*, 88.

9. Thus Fejtö, *op. cit.*, 90.

CHAPTER IV

1. R. Khevenhüller-Metsch & H. Schlitter, *Aus der Zeit Maria Theresias: Tagebuch des Fürsten J. J. Khevenhüller-Metsch, Kaiserlichen Obersthofmeisters: 1742–1776* (7 vols.) VII, 3.

2. Arneth, *Maria Theresia und Joseph*, I, 202.

3. *Ibid.*, I, 205.

4. Bibl, *op. cit.*, 79.

5. H. Marczali, *Hungary in the Eighteenth Century*, 177.

6. *Ibid.*, 188.

7. Padover, *op. cit.*, 82.

8. Mitrofanov, *op. cit.*, II, 509–511.

9. Padover, *op. cit.*, 77.

10. *Ibid.*, 72.

11. Mitrofanov, *op. cit.*, II, 153.

12. Arneth, *Maria Theresia*, IX, 90–99.

13. F. Maass, *Der Josephinismus* (5 vols.) II, 172–175.

14. Arneth, *Maria Theresia*, IX, 97.

15. Bibl, *op. cit.*, 84. Padover, *op cit.*, 73, accepts the letter as genuine and quotes from it at length.

16. Arneth, *Maria Theresia*, IX, 109.

17. R. J. Kerner, *Bohemia in the Eighteenth Century*, 35–36, 39.

18. Fejtö, *op. cit.*, 129–130.

19. *Ibid.*, 131.

20. Padover, *op. cit.*, 83.

21. Arneth, *Maria Theresia und Joseph*, I, 344.

22. *Ibid.*, I, 346.

23. *Ibid.*, I, 347.

24. *Ibid.*, I, 349.

25. *Ibid.*, I, 350–352.

26. *Ibid.*, I, 352–356; I, 358.

27. Arneth, *Maria Theresia*, IX, 349.

28. Arneth, *Maria Theresia und Joseph*, II, 5.

29. Arneth, *Maria Theresia*, IX, 357.

30. *Ibid.*, 358–359.

31. *Ibid.*, 361. Padover, *op. cit.*, 89, who concludes that "Maria Theresia emerged as a bigoted and fanatical reactionary," completely misrepresents her position in this dispute.

32. Arneth, *Maria Theresia und Joseph*, II, 81–82.

33. Arneth, *Maria Theresia*, IX, 365–369.

34. W. E. Wright, "The Initiation of Robota Abolition in Bohemia," *Journal of Central European Affairs*, XVIII, No. 3, 240.

CHAPTER V

1. Arneth, *Maria Theresia*, IX, 229–231.

2. *Ibid.*, 233–234.

3. *Ibid.*, 235–236.

4. *Ibid.*, 245–250.

5. Padover's assertion, *op. cit.*, 79, that ". . . . Joseph and the Commission organized a universal public educational system" is, to say the least, misleading.

6. See Bernard, *loc. cit.*, 43.

7. The best treatment of Sonnenfels is to be found in R. A. Kann, *A Study in Austrian Intellectual History: From Late Baroque to Romanticism.*

8. Fejtö, *op. cit.*, 146.

9. Kerner, *op. cit.*, 37.

10. H. Rieser, *Der Geist des Josefinismus*, 28–39.

11. Arneth, *Maria Theresia*, IX, 139.

12. Arneth, *Maria Theresia und Joseph*, II, 94–95.

13. *Ibid.*, II, 95–98.

14. *Ibid.*, II, 99.

15. Fejtö, *op. cit.*, 150–151.

16. Arneth, *Maria Theresia und Joseph*, II, 141–142.

17. *Ibid.*, II, 146–147.

18. *Ibid.*, II, 152.

19. *Ibid.*, II, 157–158.

20. Arneth, *Maria Theresia*, X, 62–63.

21. For the following, see Arneth, *Maria Theresia und Joseph*, II, 160–167.

22. Arneth, *Maria Theresia*, X, 70.

23. Maass, *op. cit.*, II, 219–223.

24. Fejtö, *op. cit.*, 156.

25. For details of the trip, see Arneth, *Maria Theresia und Joseph*, II, 133–139.

26. Padover, *op. cit.*, 124, speaks of ". . . . The significance of Joseph's contacts with the intellectuals . . . ," and speculates about their awareness of the great contrast between him and their own king. Unfortunately these is no evidence whatever for this.

27. Fejtö, *op. cit.*, 164.

28. Arneth, *Maria Theresia und Joseph*, II, 139.

29. *Ibid.*, II, 37, 56–58.

30. F. Schreyvogl, *Ein Jahrhundert zu früh: Das Schicksal Josephs II*, 113–122.

CHAPTER VI

1. Arneth, *Maria Theresia*, IX, 512.

2. Mitrofanov, *op. cit.*, I, 354.

3. Arneth, *Maria Theresia*, IX, 517.

4. Fejtö, *op. cit.*, 111–114.

5. For a detailed account of this meeting, and of that at Neustadt, see A. Beer, "Die Zusammenkünfte Josephs II. und Friedrichs II. zu Neisse und Neustadt," *Archiv für österreichische Geschichte*, XLVII, 1871.

6. Arneth, *Maria Theresia und Joseph*, I, 361–363.

7. For a comprehensive treatment of the Bavarian question, see my *Joseph II and Bavaria, passim.*

8. The best description of the ensuing campaign is to be found in O. Criste, *Kriege unter Kaiser Joseph II.*

9. Fejtö, *op. cit.*, 191.

CHAPTER VII

1. Arneth, *Maria Theresia und Joseph*, III, 224; Beer, *op. cit.*, 20.

2. Padover's dictum (*op. cit.*, 172) that "In all the forty years of her reign she never did a generous thing and never thought a noble thought," can only be described as grotesque.

3. Arneth, *Maria Theresia und Joseph*, III, 327.

4. Bibl, *op. cit.*, 127–128.

5. Beer, *op. cit.*, 21.

6. Fejtö, *op. cit.*, 201.

7. Padover, *op. cit.*, 172–173.

8. A. von Arneth, *Joseph II und Leopold von Toscana: Ihr Briefwechsel von 1781 bis 1740* (2 vols.) I, 36–37.

9. *Ibid.*, I, 19.

10. A. Goodwin (Ed.), *The European Nobility in the Eighteenth Century,* 104.

11. F. Walter, *Die Österreichische Zentralverwaltung: Die Zeit Josephs II. und Leopoldls II.*, 2–3.

12. E. M. Link, *The Emancipation of the Austrian Peasant: 1740–1798,* 115.

13. Walter, *op. cit.*, 24–26; Link, *op. cit.*, 116–117; Mitrofanov, *op. cit.*, I, 289.

14. Goodwin, *op. cit.*, 109.

15. Fejtö, *op. cit.*, 217, Bibl, *op. cit.*, 145–146.

CHAPTER VIII

1. Mitrofanov, *op. cit.*, II, 503.

2. Link, *op. cit.*, 120–121.

3. Mitrofanov, *op. cit.*, II, 520.

4. *Ibid.*, II, 517–519.

5. *Ibid.*, II, 521–529.

6. Link, *op. cit.*, 111–112.

7. Mitrofanov, *op. cit.*, II, 530–534.

8. Padover, *op. cit.*, 194–195.

9. Fejtö, *op. cit.*, 206–208.

10. Bibl, *op. cit.*, 171–173.

11. *Ibid.*, 165–166.

12. Mitrofanov, *op. cit.*, II, 807–819.

CHAPTER IX

1. For a detailed account of these frictions, see Maass, *op. cit.*, II, 240–250.

2. For Heinke, see *Ibid.*, II, *passim.*

3. *Ibid.*, III, 12; J. Wodka, *Kirche in Österreich*, 303.

4. Maass, *op. cit.*, II, 278–279.
5. Bibl, *op. cit.*, 180–181.
6. E. Tomek, *Kirchengeschichte Oesterreichs*, 3 vols., III, 375.
7. Kerner, *op. cit.*, 42.
8. Padover, *op. cit.*, 252–257; Marczali, *op. cit.*, 319; Tomek, *op. cit.*, III, 377.
9. Maass, *op. cit.*, IX, 63–77.
10. Tomek, *op. cit.*, III, 381–382; Wodka, *op. cit.*, 306–308; Padover, *op. cit.*, 220–227; F. Valjavec, *Der Josephinismus*, 57.
11. Padover, *op. cit.*, 225, gives this number as 27,000, which is too low.
12. Wodka, *op. cit.*, 306–308.
13. Tomek, *op. cit.*, III, 382–383.
14. Maass, *op. cit.*, II, 81 ff.; Tomek, *op. cit.*, III, 410 ff.; H. Schlitter, *Die Reise des Papstes Pius VI nach Wien*, 2–3.
15. Schlitter, *op. cit.*, 37–39.
16. A. von Arneth, *Joseph und Leopold*, I, 89–90.
17. Schlitter, *op. cit.*, 60–70.
18. *Ibid.*, 77–80.
19. Tomek, *op. cit.*, III, 429–430; Maass, *op. cit.*, II, 191.

CHAPTER X

1. Link, *op. cit.*, 105–110.
2. Kerner, *op. cit.*, 43.
3. Marczali, *op. cit.*, 190.
4. Mitrofanov, *op. cit.*, II, 606.
5. Link, *op. cit.*, 130.
6. Wright, *loc. cit.*, 248–249; Fejtö, *op. cit.*, 271–275.
7. Link, *op. cit.*, 135.
8. Kerner, *op. cit.*, 44.
9. Mitrofanov, *op. cit.*, II, 471–472.
10. Link, *op. cit.*, 139–140.
11. Kerner, *op. cit.*, 45.
12. Marczali, *op. cit.*, 90.
13. H. Freudenberger, "Industrialization in Bohemia and Moravia in the Eighteenth Century," *Journal of Central European Affairs*, XIX, January 1960, 349–350.
14. Goodwin, *op. cit.*, 105; Kerner, *op. cit.*, 47.
15. Padover, *op. cit.*, 302–303.
16. *Ibid.*, 270–271.
17. Leopold's secret journal was discovered and deciphered by Adam Wandruszka. See his *Leopold II* (2 vols.) I, 342–348.

CHAPTER XI

1. Arneth, *Joseph und Leopold*, I, 115–124; Fejtö, *op. cit.*, 247–249.
2. A. von Arneth, *Joseph II. und Katharina von Russland*, 169–173.
3. Bernard, *Joseph II and Bavaria*, 165 ff., 189–192.
4. Arneth, *Joseph und Leopold*, II, 81.
5. A. Beer & J. Fiedler, *Joseph II. und Graf Ludwig Cobenzl: Ihr Briefwechsel*, (2 vols.) II, 150–155.
6. *Ibid.*, II, 156–160.
7. See H. Schlitter, *Die Regierung Josephs II. in den Österreichischen Niederlanden*, and O. Lorenz, *Joseph II. und die Belgische Revolution*.
8. Arneth, *Joseph und Katharina*, 185 ff.

9. Criste, *op. cit.*, 144 ff.

10. Arneth, *Joseph und Leopold*, II, 265; Beer & Friedler, *Joseph und Cobenzl*, II, 361.

11. H. H. von der Burg, *Gestalten und Ideen: Karl Joseph Fürst de Ligne*, 88.

Selected Bibliography

I PRINTED SOURCE MATERIALS

The most important collections of letters and documents for the life of Joseph are thē following:

Arneth, A. von. *Marie Antoinette, Joseph II. und Leopold II.: Ihr Briefwechsel.* Leipzig, Paris, Wien: 1866.

Arneth, A. von. *Joseph II. und Katharina von Russland: Ihr Briefwechsel.* Wien: 1869.

Arneth, A. von. *Die Relationen der Botschafter Venedigs über Österreich im achtzehnten Jahrhundert. Fontes Rerum Austriacarum II, Diplomataria* XXII. Wien: 1863.

Arneth, A. von. *Maria Theresia und Joseph II.: Ihre Correspondenz sammt Briefen Joseph's an seinen Bruder Leopold.* 3 vols. Wien: 1867, 1868.

Arneth, A. von. *Joseph II. und Leopold von Toscana: Ihr Briefwechsel von 1781 bis 1790.* 2 vols. Wien: 1872.

Arneth, A. von. *Briefe der Kaiserin Maria Theresia an Ihre Kinder und Freunde.* 4 vols. Wien: 1881.

Arneth, A. von & Flammermont, J. *Correspondance secrète du Comte de Mercy-Argenteau avec l'Empereur Joseph II. et le Prince de Kaunitz.* 2 vols. Paris: 1889.

Arneth, A. von & M. A. Geffroy. *Correspondance secrète entre Marie Thérèse et le Cte. de Mercy-Argenteau, avec les lettres de Marie-Thérèse et de Marie Antoinette.* 3 vols. Paris: 1874.

Beer, A. *Joseph II., Leopold II. und Kaunitz: Ihr Briefwechsel.* Wien: 1873.

Beer, A. & J. von Fiedler. *Joseph II. und Graf Ludwig Cobenzl: Ihr Briefwechsel. Fontes Rerum Austriacarum II.* Nos. 53, 54. 2 vols. Wien: 1901.

Brunner, S. *Correspondances intimes de l'Empereur Joseph II, avec son ami le Comte de Cobenzl et son prémier ministre le Prince de Kaunitz.* Mainz, Paris, Bruxelles: 1871.

Christoph, P. (Pseud.) *Maria Theresia und Marie Antoinette: Ihr geheimer Briefwechsel.* Wien: 1952.

Khevenhüller-Metsch, J. J. *Aus der Zeit Maria Theresias. Tagebuch des fürsten Johann Josef Khevenhüller-Metsch, Kaiserlichen obersthofmeisters 1742–76.* Edited by R. Khevenhüller-Metsch and H. Schlitter. 7 vols. Vienna: 1907–25.

Schlitter, H. *Kaunitz, Philipp Cobenzl und Spielmann: Ihr Briefwechsel (1779–1792).* Wien: 1899.

II BIOGRAPHIES OF JOSEPH

Benedikt, E. *Kaiser Joseph II. 1741–1790. Mit Benützung ungedruckter Quellen.* Wien: 1936. Based on the sources but impressionistic.

Bibl, V. *Kaiser Joseph II.: Ein Vorkämpfer der Grossdeutschen Idee.* Wien & Leipzig: 1943. Joseph seen as a German national hero.

Bright, J. F. *Joseph II.* London: 1897. Slight and antiquated.

Fejtö, F. *Un Habsbourg révolutionnaire: Joseph II.* Paris: 1953. Makes use of little-known and valuable materials, particularly about Joseph's relations with Hungary, but unfortunately dispenses with all source references.

Mitrofanov. P. von. *Joseph II. Seine politische und kulturelle Tätigkeit.* Trans. by V. von Demelic. 2 vols. Wien & Leipzig: 1910. Not really a biography, but a still indispensable description of the Josephinian system.

Padover, S. K. *The Revolutionary Emperor: Joseph the Second, 1741–1790.* New York: 1934. The life of Joseph in English, but not free from major errors, both of fact and interpretation.

Schreyvogl, F. *Ein Jahrhundert zu früh: Das Schicksal Josephs II.* Wien, Berlin, Stuttgart: 1964. The most recent life, semi-popular, and without any strikingly new interpretations.

III REFORMS: ADMINISTRATIVE, JUDICIAL, AGRARIAN AND SOCIAL

Freudenberger, H. "Industrialization in Bohemia and Moravia in the Eighteenth Century." *Journal of Central European Affairs,* XIX, Jaunary 1960.

Goodwin, A. (Ed.) *The European Nobility in the Eighteenth Century.* London: 1953.

Grünberg, K., *Die Baunerbefreiung und die Auflösung des gutsherrlich-bäuerlichen Verhältnisses in Böhmen, Mähren and Schlesien.* 2 vols. Leipzig: 1893–94.

Kerner, R. J. *Bohemia in the Eighteenth Century.* New York: 1932.

Link, E. M. *The Emancipation of the Austrian Peasant 1740–1798.* New York: 1949.

Marczali, H. *Hungary in the Eighteenth Century.* Cambridge: 1910.

Walter, F. *Die Österreichische Zentralverwaltung: II/I/2/1. Die Zeit Josephs II. und Leopolds II. (1780–1792).* Wien: 1950.

Walter, F. *Männer um Maria Theresia.* Wien: 1951.

Wright, W. E. *Serf, Seigneur and Sovereign.* Minneapolis: 1966.

IV RELIGIOUS REFORMS, CULTURAL AND INTELLECTUAL LIFE

H. Benedikt, "Der Josephinismus vor Joseph II." *Österreich und Europa.* Graz, Wien, Köln: 1965.

Bernard, P. P. "The Origins of Josephinism: Two Studies." *The Colorado College Studies.* VII, February 1964.

Franz, H. *Die Zensur unter Joseph II.* Strasbourg: 1911.

Hazard, P. *European Thought in the Eighteenth Century.* English translation, London: 1954.

Holzknecht, G. *Ursprung und Herkunft der Reformideen Kaiser Josefs II. auf kirchlichem Gebiete.* Innsbruck: 1914.

Kann, R. A. *A Study in Austrian Intellectual History: From Late Baroque to Romanticism.* New York: 1960.

Maass, F. *Der Josephinismus: Ursprung und Wesen.* 5 vols. Wien: 1951–1961.

Müller, W. *Gerhard van Swieten.* Wien: 1883.

Rieser, H. *Der Geist des Josephinismus.* Wien: 1963.

Sashegyi, O. *Zensur und Geistesfreiheit unter Joseph II.* Budapest: 1958.

Schlitter, H. *Die Reise des Papstes Pius VI. nach Wien und sein Aufenthalt Daselbst.* Wien: 1892.

Tomek, E. *Kirchengeschichte Oesterreichs.* 3 vols. Innsbruck: 1938–58.

Valjavec, F. *Der Josephinismus.* 2nd Ed. Munich: 1945.

Wangermann, E. *From Joseph II to the Jacobin Trials.* Oxford: 1959.

Winter, E. *Der Josefinismus.* 2nd Ed. Berlin: 1962.

Wodka, J. *Kirche in Österreich.* Wien: 1959.

E. Zöllner, "Bemerkungen zum Problem der Beziehungen zwischen Aufklärung und Josephinismus." *Österreich und Europa.* Graz, Wien, Köln: 1965.

V FOREIGN AFFAIRS AND WAR

Beer, A. *Die orientalische Politik Oesterreichs seit 1774.* Prague & Leipzig: 1883.

Bernard, P. P. *Joseph II and Bavaria.* The Hague: 1965.

Criste, O. *Kriege unter Kaiser Joseph II.* Wien: 1904.

Hanfstaengl, E. F. S. *Amerika und Europa von Marlborough bis Mirabeau.* München: 1930.

Lorenz, O. *Joseph II und die Belgische Revolution.* Wien: 1862.

Nosinich, J. *Kaiser Joseph II. als Staatsmann und Feldherr: Österreichs Politik und Kriege in dem Jahren 1763 bis 1790.* 3 vols. Wien: 1882–1885.

Pichler, K. *Die Beziehungen zwischen Österreich und Frankreich innerhalb der Jahre 1780–1790.* Znaim: 1897.

Regele, O. *Der Österreichische Hofkriegsrat: 1556–1848.* Wien: 1949.

Schlitter, H. *Die Regierung Josefs II. in den Österreichischen Niederlanden.* Wien: 1900.

Temperley, H. W. V. *Frederick the Great and Kaiser Joseph: An Episode of War and Diplomacy in the Eighteenth Century.* London: 1915.

H. Wagner, "Die Reise Joseph II. nach Frankreich 1777 und die Reformen in Österreich," *Österreich und Europa.* Graz, Wien, Köln: 1965.

Wolf, G. *Oesterreich und Preussen (1780–1790).* Wien: 1880.

VI OTHER WORKS

Arneth, A. von. *Geschichte Maria Theresias,* 10 vols. Wien: 1863–1879.

Guglia, E. *Maria Theresia,* 2 vols. Munich & Berlin: 1917.

Hennings, F. *Und Sitzet zur linken Hand: Franz Stephan von Lothringen.* Wien, Berlin, Stuttgart: 1961.

Küntzel, G. *Fürst Kaunitz-Rittberg als Staatsmann.* Frankfurt/a M.: 1923.

Mikoletsky, H. L. *Kaiser Franz I. Stephan und der Ursprung des Hapsburgisch-Lothringischen Familienvermögens.* München: 1961.

Novotny, A. *Staatskanzler Kaunitz als geistige Persönlichkeit.* Wien: 1934.

Palmer, R. R. *The Age of Democratic Revolution.* Vol. I. Princeton, N. J.: 1959.

Von Der Burg, H. H. *Karl Joseph Fürst de Ligne.* Graz, Wien, Köln: 1965.

Wandruszka, A. *Leopold II.* 2 vols. Wien und München: 1963, 1965.

Index

DATE DUE

FEB 10 '70 NOV 14 '88		
FEB 24 '70		
NOV 2 '70		
FEB 7 '72		
MAR 23 '76		
OCT 14 '76		
FE 17 '77		
AP 7 '77		
MR 23 '81		
FE 24 '82		
FE 17 '83		
MR 2 '83		
OC 11 '83		
FEB 7 '85		
FE 27 '85		
MAR 3 '88		
MAR 22 '88		
APR 4 '88		